2R EUREKA!

Success in Science

Carol Chapman
Rob Musker
Daniel Nicholson
Moira Sheehan

Heinemann

Heinemann Educational Publishers
Halley Court, Jordan Hill, Oxford, OX2 8EJ
a division of Reed Educational & Professional Publishing Ltd
Heinemann is a registered trademark of Reed Educational & Professional Publishing Ltd

OXFORD MELBOURNE AUCKLAND
JOHANNESBURG BLANTYRE GABORONE
IBADAN PORTSMOUTH NH (USA) CHICAGO

First published 2001

ISBN 0 435 57627 5

05 04 03 02
10 9 8 7 6 5 4

Edited by Ruth Holmes

Designed and typeset by Ken Vail Graphic Design, Cambridge

Original illustration © Heinemann Educational Publishers 2001

Illustrated by Graham-Cameron Illustration (Harriet Buckley, Sarah Wimperis), SGA (Stephen Sweet), Nick Hawken, Margaret Jones, B L Kearley Ltd. (Shirley Bellwood), David Lock, Richard Morris, Sylvie Poggio Artists Agency (Tim Davies).

Printed and bound in Spain by Edelvives

Picture research by Jennifer Johnson

Acknowledgments
The authors and publishers would like to thank the following for permission to use copyright material:
extract p2, Dispatch, spring 1996 volume VII, No 1; **extract p18,** Daily Mail 13/3/99, **extract p106,** Birmingham Evening Mail 8/12/98.

The publishers have made every effort to trace the copyright holders, but if they have inadvertently overlooked any, they will be pleased to make the necessary arrangements at the first opportunity.

For photograph acknowledgements, please see page 154.

Tel: 01865 888058 www.heinemann.co.uk

Everyone can

Understand science by

Reading this book, be

Enthralled, become

Knowledgeable and

Achieve success…

…with EUREKA!

Welcome to *Eureka! Success in Science*

This is the second of three books designed to help you learn all the science ideas you need during Key Stage 3. We hope you'll enjoy the books as well as learning a lot from them.

These two pages will help you get the most out of the book so it's worth spending a couple of minutes reading them!

This book has nine units which each cover a different topic. The units have three types of pages:

Setting the scene

Each unit starts with a double-page spread which reminds you of what you know already about the topic. They tell you other interesting things, such as the place of science in everyday life and the history of some science inventions and ideas.

Learn about

► Energy

Most of the double-page spreads in a unit introduce and explain new ideas about the topic. They start with a list of these so that you can see what you are going to learn about.

Think about

► Fair tests

► Variables

Each unit has a double-page spread called Think about. You will work in pairs or small groups and discuss your answers to the questions. These pages will help you understand how scientists work and how ideas about science develop.

On the pages there are these symbols:

ⓐ Make a list of foods that give you a lot of energy.

Quick questions scattered through the pages help you check your knowledge and understanding of the ideas as you go along.

Questions

The questions at the end of the spread help you check you understand all the important ideas.

For your notes

These list the important ideas from the spread to help you learn, write notes and revise.

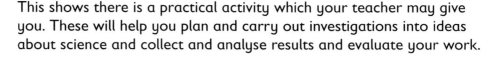

 This shows there is a practical activity which your teacher may give you. These will help you plan and carry out investigations into ideas about science and collect and analyse results and evaluate your work.

 This shows there is an ICT activity which your teacher may give you. You will use computers to collect results from datalogging experiments, or work with spreadsheets and databases, or get useful information from CD-ROMS or the Internet.

 This shows there is a writing activity which your teacher may give you to help you write about the science you learn.

 This shows there is a discussion activity which your teacher may give you. You will share your ideas about science with others in a discussion.

At the back of the book:

 All the important scientific words in the text appear in **bold** type. They are listed with their meanings in the Glossary at the back of the book. Look there to remind yourself what they mean.

 There is an index at the very back of the book, where you can find out which pages cover a particular topic.

Activities to check your learning

Your teacher may give you these activities:

Lift-off!
When you start a unit, this short exercise reminds you what you already know about a topic.

Unit map
You can use this to think about what you already know about a topic. You can also use it to revise a topic before a test or exam.

Quiz
You can use the quiz at the end of each unit to see what you are good at and what you might need to revise.

Revision 1
You can use the revision sheets to revise a part of a unit which you aren't so good at.

End of unit test
This helps you and your teacher check what you learned during the unit, and measures your progress and success.

Contents

Introduction iv

1 Acids and bases

1.1 Acid accident 2
1.2 Acids, bases and alkalis 4
1.3 How acidic? 6
1.4 Cancelling out acidity 8
1.5 Salt on your chips, Sir? 10
1.6 Corrosion 12
1.7 Acid in the air 14
T 1.8 The answer lies in the soil 16

2 Vital organs

2.1 New lungs for Leann 18
2.2 Right for the job 20
2.3 An organised system 22
2.4 Bones and joints 24
2.5 A moving tale 26
T 2.6 Examining Tharg 28

3 Earth and space

3.1 One small step for man 30
3.2 Round the Sun 32
3.3 Shedding light on things 34
3.4 Picturing the Solar System 36
3.5 All in a day 38
3.6 All in a year 40
3.7 In orbit 42
T 3.8 Making models 44

4 Matter

4.1 It's atomic 46
4.2 Making new materials 48
4.3 All change! 50
4.4 Wandering particles 52
4.5 Size matters 54
4.6 Under pressure 56
4.7 Solubility 58
T 4.8 Scientific models 60

5 Nutrition

5.1 Organically grown 62
5.2 What's in food? 64
5.3 Balanced diet 66
5.4 The digestive system 68
5.5 Enzymes 70
5.6 Food for energy 72
T 5.7 Chewing it over 74

6 Energy resources

6.1 The right fuel for the job 76
6.2 Fossil fuels 78
6.3 Burn it! 80
6.4 Electricity from fossil fuels 82
6.5 Turning the turbine 84
6.6 More turbines turning 86
6.7 Getting around 88
T 6.8 How many? 90

7 Rocks

7.1 Earth detectives. 92

7.2 Rock breaking 94

7.3 Disappearing rocks 96

7.4 Transporting rock 98

7.5 Making rocks 100

7.6 Rock types 102

T **7.7** Name that rock. 104

8 Environment

8.1 No relief road!. 106

8.2 Putting plants into groups. 108

8.3 Plants go for energy 110

8.4 Growing and growing. 112

8.5 Home alone? 114

8.6 Food for thought. 116

T **8.7** Special daisies 118

9 Light and sound

9.1 Flashes and bangs 120

9.2 Travelling light. 122

9.3 Which ray? 124

9.4 Bending light 126

9.5 Coloured light 128

T **9.6** Colour combinations 130

9.7 Sound is like light. 132

9.8 Sound is different from light . . . 134

Glossary 136

Index 146

T indicates Think about spread

Acid accident

Runaway Train Derails, Spills Sulfuric Acid down Mountainside

A runaway train derailed in the pre-dawn hours in Leadville, Colorado, killing two railroad employees and injuring a third. The February accident sent a river of sulfuric acid down a snowy mountainside and across a highway.

Why is sulfuric acid dangerous?

Concentrated sulfuric acid is **corrosive**. This means that it eats away most of the materials it touches, including human flesh! All corrosive substances have a warning label. These labels are used by the emergency services to help them decide how to manage an accident.

A solution

An **acid** is a solution of a particular kind of solid or gas in water. An acid that does not contain much water is a **concentrated** acid. An acid that contains quite a lot of water is called a **dilute** acid. In the Leadville accident, the snow melted and diluted the acid a little. Very dilute sulfuric acid is not corrosive.

Toxic means poisonous. Sulfuric acid is not labelled toxic.

According to witnesses, sulfuric acid flowed downhill in 'three or four streams', flooding across the highway and forming pools in a parking lot on the other side of the road. Fortunately the acid did not reach the nearby Eagle River, which is the municipal water supply for several communities.

Dozens of drivers and rescue workers sought treatment at nearby medical facilities for exposure to fumes, with symptoms such as burning eyes, shortness of breath and nausea. Sulfuric acid is a corrosive acid that is highly poisonous by inhalation and causes severe burns in contact with skin tissue. Vapours are irritating to the eyes and throat.

The Mintern Fire Department was first on the scene.

Two million pounds of soda ash and lime, needed to neutralise the acid, were brought in by truck and rail. Hulcher Professional Services of Rapid City brought in heavy equipment to clear wreckage from the tracks. The acid-tainted snow was collected and removed from the mountain.

TOXIC
poisonous

a Read the newspaper extracts again. Find the word that has been used wrongly to describe sulfuric acid, and explain why it is inaccurate. Suggest a better word to replace it.

Useful acids

Sulfuric acid is a useful acid. For example, it is used in car batteries. You need to handle it carefully to avoid burning holes in your clothes or your skin.

We use products that contain acids every day, and not all of them are dangerous. Many acids are not corrosive – they do not burn or eat things away. This may be because they have been diluted with water. Vinegar is safe, but concentrated ethanoic acid, the acid contained in vinegar, is very corrosive.

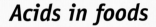

Vinegar contains ethanoic acid.

Acids in foods

Look at the photos. Many of the foods we eat contain acids. Some acids have very long names, but the word 'acid' is part of the name.

Your stomach also has acid in it. The acid helps to digest your food. Too much stomach acid gives you indigestion. You can take tablets to treat the indigestion.

b Tablets for indigestion are called anti-acid tablets. What does the name tell you about how they work?

c Look at the pictures of foods and the acids they contain. Make a list of all the acids you can think of that are found in foods or drinks. What sort of taste do some of them have?

lactic acid

ascorbic acid, which is vitamin C

tannic acid

citric acid

Questions

1. Make a list of the possible effects of sulfuric acid on the body.

2. Predict what might happen if sulfuric acid got into the community water supply.

3. Explain the advantages and disadvantages of the weather conditions on the day of the Colorado acid spill.

4. What do you think would happen if a tanker spilled acid on a motorway in this country in the summer? Suggest a sequence of events.

5. Calculate how much water would be needed by the fire service to dilute a 500-litre acid spill by four times.

6. Explain why battery acid has a corrosive hazard label but cola drinks do not.

7. Lynn and Ryan were arguing. Lynn said that all acids are corrosive. Ryan said they're not. Who was right? Explain your answer.

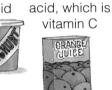

Did you know?

Rhubarb stalks are safe to eat, but the leaves contain poisonous oxalic acid. This puts animals off eating them!

Acids, bases and alkalis

Acids

Some acids are in foods. They have a sour taste. Other acids may be **corrosive**, **toxic**, **harmful** or **irritant**. Hazard warning labels are used on their containers to warn people of the dangers.

Some insects and even some plants have acidic stings which they use to attack animals that try to eat them. Nettles have stinging hairs on their leaves and stems. When an animal touches the hairs they break off, releasing the acid which causes the sting.

a Ants have acidic stings. When do you think ants use their stings?

Bases and alkalis

Look at the photo showing substances found in the kitchen or bathroom. They all contain **bases**. A base is the opposite of an acid – it cancels out acidity.

Some bases dissolve in water. We call these **alkalis**. Like acids, many alkalis are corrosive.

b Explain what alkalis and bases have in common and how they differ.

Learn about

▶ Acids, bases and alkalis

▶ Indicators

CORROSIVE
may destroy living tissues on contact

TOXIC
poisonous

HARMFUL
may have health risk if breathed in, taken internally or absorbed through skin

IRRITANT
non-corrosive substance which can cause red or blistered skin

Hair relaxers

If you have very curly or wavy hair, you can straighten it using chemical relaxers. The most common ones contain an alkali called sodium hydroxide. There is a risk that sodium hydroxide may burn, break or damage the hair. The stronger the solution, the faster it works, so it must be used carefully. Chemical hair relaxers should be applied by a professional hair stylist.

c Which hazard warning label would you expect to find on a packet of hair relaxer?

Safety first

The acids in food taste sour, but you must never taste a substance to find out whether it is an acid. You would know if you had spilled a corrosive acid on yourself as it would burn, whereas an alkali would feel soapy. However, you must never touch a substance to find out if it is an alkali. Many acids and alkalis are dangerous because they are corrosive.

Indicators

Using your senses is not a safe way of finding out whether a solution is acidic or alkaline. The best way is to use an **indicator**. An indicator is a coloured substance that shows you whether the solution you are testing is an acid, an alkali or **neutral**. A neutral solution is neither acidic nor alkaline. Pure water is neutral. You can make an indicator using colours from flowers, fruits and vegetables. When an indicator is mixed with an acid or alkali, it will change colour.

Did you know?

Hydrangea plants change colour in acidic and alkaline soil. They are blue in acidic soils and pink in alkaline soils. This is the opposite of what you would expect with litmus!

Using litmus

Litmus is an indicator made from lichens. We use it in laboratories to find out whether solutions are acidic, alkaline or neutral.

- Litmus paper comes in small strips.
- You can use blue litmus paper or red litmus paper.
- To test a solution, dip a glass rod into it.
- Touch the litmus paper with the glass rod.

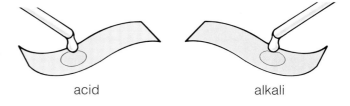

acid   alkali

Acids turn blue litmus paper red. Alkalis turn red litmus paper blue. Both blue and red litmus paper stay the same colour with neutral solutions.

Did you know?

Red cabbage acts as an indicator. It turns bright red in acid, and blue in alkali.

Questions

1. What is an indicator? Explain what indicators are used for.

2. What safety precautions would you need to take if you were a hair stylist using alkaline hair relaxers?

3. Draw a table to show the colours you would expect to see if you put an acidic, an alkaline and a neutral solution on red litmus and on blue litmus.

4. Look carefully at the table which shows some of the indicators you might find in a paint factory laboratory.

Indicator	Acidic	Alkaline	Neutral
Phenolphthalein	Clear	Red	Clear
Methyl orange	Red	Yellow	Yellow
Methyl red	Pink	Yellow	Yellow

Which indicator would show the difference between an alkaline solution and a neutral solution the best? Explain your answer.

For your notes

Acids can taste sour. Acids may be corrosive, poisonous, harmful or irritant.

Bases are the opposites of acids. They cancel out acidity.

An **alkali** is a soluble base. Alkalis can feel soapy. Alkalis may be corrosive, poisonous, harmful or irritant.

A **neutral** solution is neither acidic nor alkaline.

Indicators turn different colours with acidic, alkaline and neutral solutions.

How acidic?

Universal indicator

Litmus is very useful for telling whether a substance is acidic or alkaline, but it does not tell you how strong or weak it is or how dangerous it is. **Universal indicator** is a mixture of indicators made from plants. Because it is a mixture of indicators it can produce a range of colours. It will show a different colour for different strengths of acidic or alkaline solutions.

- Universal indicator comes in liquid or paper form.
- To use universal indicator liquid, add two drops to the solution you want to test.
- To use universal indicator paper, dip a glass rod into the solution. Touch the indicator paper with the glass rod.
- Compare the colour with the chart.

a Give two reasons why universal indicator is more useful than litmus.

The pH scale

Some acidic solutions are strongly acidic, and others are weakly acidic. The same is true for alkaline solutions. We use pH numbers to measure the strength of the acidity or alkalinity. (Remember to write it with a small 'p' and capital 'H'.) A neutral solution has pH 7. Acidic solutions have a pH less than 7. The lower the pH, the stronger the acidity. Look at the **pH scale** at the top of the next page. Hydrochloric acid is strongly acidic, with pH 1. Vinegar is more weakly acidic, with pH 3–4. Alkaline solutions have a pH greater than 7. Sodium hydroxide solution is strongly alkaline, with pH 14. Ammonia is more weakly alkaline, with pH 11.

Solutions of acids and alkalis can be **concentrated** or **dilute**. If you add water to a concentrated solution of an acid, it becomes more dilute.

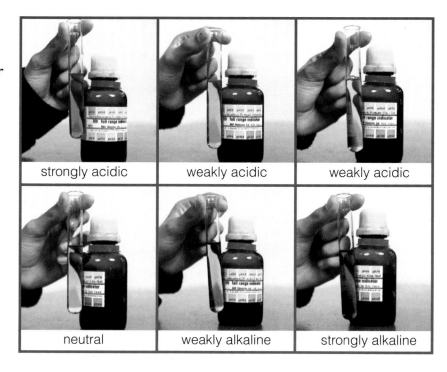

| strongly acidic | weakly acidic | weakly acidic |
| neutral | weakly alkaline | strongly alkaline |

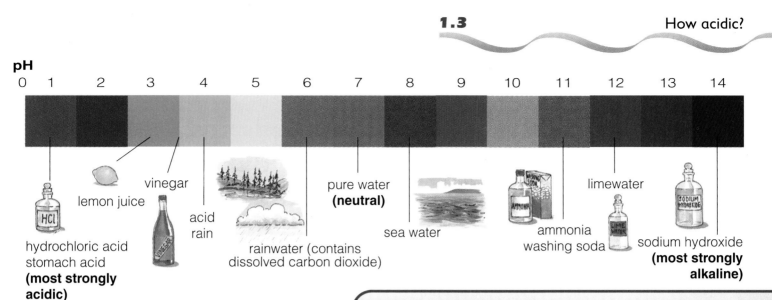

pH
0 1 2 3 4 5 6 7 8 9 10 11 12 13 14

lemon juice
vinegar
acid rain
rainwater (contains dissolved carbon dioxide)
pure water **(neutral)**
sea water
ammonia washing soda
limewater
sodium hydroxide **(most strongly alkaline)**
hydrochloric acid stomach acid **(most strongly acidic)**

b The pH of milk is 6.5. What colour would universal indicator turn with milk?

Did you know?

In the food industry, technicians test the pH of the products. They need to advise the packaging department about whether the food is likely to be corrosive. This helps them decide what sort of container to put it in.

Questions

1. Look very carefully at the pH chart. Copy the table and complete it. The first line has been done for you.

Liquid	Colour with universal indicator	pH	Description
Indigestion medicine		9	Weakly alkaline
Tea			
Salt water			
Rainwater			
Soap			
Lemon juice			

2. During a long-distance space mission, one of the astronauts is suspected to have an unusual viral illness. The virus produces an acidic substance in the saliva.

   a Explain how you could use universal indicator paper to check whether any of the other crew members have contracted the disease.

   Some of the medical staff claim that the pH test is unreliable because it will give a false positive result if the patient has been eating certain fruits.

   b How could the test be made more reliable?

3. Why would universal indicator be more useful than litmus if you were working in a food technology laboratory?

4. Design an illustrated flow chart for a technician which shows at a glance how to use universal indicator paper.

For your notes

An acidic solution may be strongly or weakly acidic. An alkaline solution may be strongly or weakly alkaline.

A **concentrated** acid or alkali becomes more **dilute** if you add water.

Universal indicator turns different colours with different strengths of acidity and alkalinity.

The **pH scale** is used to measure the strengths of acidic and alkaline solutions.

Water is neutral, so it has pH 7.

Cancelling out acidity

Putting them together

We say that a base is the opposite of an acid, because if you add a base to an acid you take away its acidity and make a new substance.

If you add vinegar to the base sodium hydrogencarbonate, you will see bubbles. The vinegar, which is an acid, is reacting with the base. New substances are being formed. We say that a chemical reaction has taken place. The reaction is irreversible. You cannot get the vinegar or the sodium hydrogencarbonate back.

When an acid reacts with a base, the chemical reaction that takes place is called **neutralisation**. Remember, a base that will dissolve in water is called an alkali. So all alkalis dissolve in water, and they also neutralise acids.

ⓐ Why is neutralisation described as an irreversible reaction?

Learn about

➤ Neutralisation

Acid indigestion

Your stomach makes hydrochloric acid which helps to digest your food. The stomach has a special layer which stops the acid corroding your insides! Sometimes the stomach produces too much acid and you might get acid indigestion. This happens because you have eaten too much, not because you have eaten acidic food.

Indigestion remedies are sometimes called 'antacids' or 'anti-acids'. They have alkalis or bases in them to neutralise the stomach acid. Before all these medicines were available, people just used to take a spoonful of sodium hydrogencarbonate in a glass of water. It was cheap and it worked!

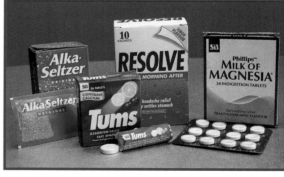

Toothpaste

Inside your mouth, there are lots of bacteria which feed on the food remains left on your teeth. They produce acid. Your teeth are covered with a substance called enamel, which is the hardest substance in your body, but it can still be attacked by acids. Toothpaste is a base. It helps to neutralise the acids produced by bacteria and acids in your food.

Problem soil

Some soils are slightly acidic. This is fine for plants such as heathers, which grow in places like the Yorkshire moors. The rhododendrons in the photo also like acidic soil. But most plants and food crops will not grow in acidic soil. The acid stops the bacteria in the soil breaking down the dead plants properly. This stops the water draining away and the soil becomes waterlogged. Peat bogs have very wet, acidic soil. Farmers and gardeners dig in a base called **lime** to neutralise the acidic soil.

Sting relief

A bee sting is acidic. You can relieve the pain with sodium hydrogencarbonate or calamine lotion, which will neutralise the sting. A wasp sting is alkaline.

b Which substances would you find at home to treat a wasp sting?

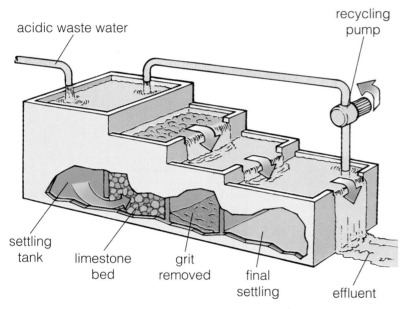

acidic waste water
recycling pump
settling tank
limestone bed
grit removed
final settling
effluent

Industrial effluent

Water from factories is sometimes contaminated with acids or alkalis. At the water treatment works, a stream of alkaline water may be mixed with a stream of acidic waste water so that they neutralise each other. Lime may be added to acidic waste water to neutralise the acid, and then left to settle out. Alternatively, the acidic water is passed over limestone, as shown.

Alkaline water is neutralised by adding acid or bubbling carbon dioxide through it to form carbonic acid.

c What could happen if acids or alkalis from factories leaked into our rivers?

Questions

1. Explain why alkalis are often described as the opposites of acids.

2. What happens when sodium hydrogencarbonate is added to vinegar? What do you see?

3. Val had acid indigestion. Roger told her not to drink cola. Why do you think he did this? What should she do?

4. What would you do to neutralise an acidic soil? How would you test to see if the neutralisation has worked?

5. If your neighbour wanted her hydrangeas to be pink not blue, which substance should she dig into the soil?

6. How is alkaline industrial waste water neutralised?

For your notes

When you add a base to an acid, a chemical reaction called **neutralisation** takes place.

Salt on your chips, Sir?

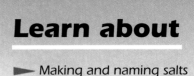

Making a salt

Sodium hydroxide is an alkali. If you take solutions of hydrochloric acid and sodium hydroxide that have the same concentration, and mix equal volumes of them, the sodium hydroxide neutralises the acid. If you test the solution with universal indicator paper, you will find it has pH 7.

If you leave the solution to evaporate, you will see crystals of salt. Yes, this is the salt you put on your chips! But, remember you must never taste anything in a laboratory.

Neutralisation

When an acid is neutralised by a base, a salt and water are made. In science a **salt** is a substance we get from neutralisation. There are lots of different salts. In the reaction between hydrochloric acid and sodium hydroxide, sodium chloride (common salt) and water are made. You can write a word equation for this reaction:

hydrochloric acid + sodium hydroxide ⟶ sodium chloride + water

Hydrochloric acid and sodium hydroxide are the substances that reacted. We call them the reactants. We call the substances that are made in a chemical reaction the products. Sodium chloride and water are the products.

Datalogging

It is important to use the correct amounts of acid and alkali in a neutralisation reaction. You can use an indicator or a pH meter to test for neutralisation. The photo shows Hassan and Martin using a pH sensor and datalogger to monitor the reaction.

At the start, they put $50\,cm^3$ of sodium hydroxide solution in the flask. They used a burette to add hydrochloric acid to the alkali, drop by drop. The volume of acid needed to neutralise $50\,cm^3$ of alkali was $5\,cm^3$. Then they continued to add the acid until the pH became steady again.

The graph they displayed at the end is shown here.

a How did they know when neutralisation was complete?

b They concluded that the hydrochloric acid was 10 times more concentrated than the alkali. Explain how they worked this out this from their results.

c What is the pH of the hydrochloric acid?

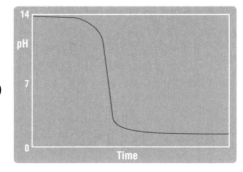

Making other salts

If you use other acids and alkalis, you get different salts. We can write a general word equation for the neutralisation reaction:

> acid + base → salt + water
> **reactants**   **products**

To name a salt, start by taking the name of the metal from the base. The second part comes from the acid – hydrochloric acid makes **chlorides** and sulfuric acid makes **sulfates**. The salt formed when you mix calcium carbonate and sulfuric acid is called calcium sulfate.

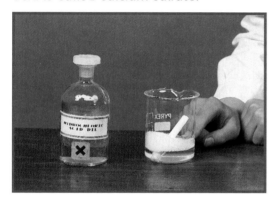

Making fertilisers

Some salts are found in rocks. We get sodium chloride from the ground as rock salt. Other salts have to be made in factories. Large amounts of ammonium nitrate and ammonium sulfate are made in factories. These salts are used as fertilisers for growing crops. Ammonium sulfate is made by neutralising sulfuric acid. Ammonium nitrate is made by neutralising nitric acid:

> nitric acid + ammonium hydroxide → ammonium nitrate + water
> **reactants**   **products**

Chalk and acids

Chalk is **calcium carbonate**. Carbonates are bases, so they neutralise acids to make salts.

If you take a piece of chalk and drop it into hydrochloric acid, as shown in the photo, you will see bubbles of carbon dioxide gas:

> calcium carbonate + hyrochloric acid → calcium chloride + water + carbon dioxide

We can write a general word equation for the reaction between an acid and a carbonate:

> acid + carbonate → salt + water + carbon dioxide

Questions

1. Explain how you can make a sample of common salt in the laboratory.

2. What are the products in a neutralisation reaction between an acid and a base?

3. Write word equations to show how:
   a ammonium sulfate fertiliser could be produced
   b calcium carbonate reacts with hydrochloric acid.

4. Copy and complete these word equations.
   a hydrochloric acid + magnesium hydroxide → _____ + water
   b hydrochloric acid + _____ → zinc chloride + _____
   c _____ + calcium hydroxide → calcium sulfate + _____
   d sulfuric acid + _____ → sodium sulfate + _____

5. Which do you think is more accurate for monitoring a neutralisation reaction, an indicator or a pH sensor? Explain your answer.

For your notes

When an acid is neutralised by a base, a **salt** and water are formed.

The name of the salt comes from the names of the acid and the base used to make it.

Carbonates neutralise acids, forming a salt, water and carbon dioxide gas.

11

Corrosion

Hubble, bubble!

Some acids attack metals like iron and zinc. When a chemical eats away at a solid like this, we call it **corrosion**. Some metals are corroded faster than others.

A closer look at zinc

Zinc reacts faster than some metals. If you add a few granules of zinc to some sulfuric acid in a beaker, it fizzes. The zinc is corroded and bubbles form. When all of the zinc has reacted, the bubbles stop.

Acids react with some metals to make a salt and **hydrogen** gas. We can write a general word equation:

> acid + metal → salt + hydrogen
> **reactants** **products**

a Which salt is made when zinc reacts with sulfuric acid?

The word equation for the reaction between zinc and sulfuric acid is:

> sulfuric acid + zinc → zinc sulfate + hydrogen

Different metals

Jade and Itora did an experiment to investigate what happens when different metal powders are added to dilute sulfuric acid.

b Which metal reacted most quickly with sulfuric acid?

c What do the results tell you about iron?

d Which metal did not react with sulfuric acid?

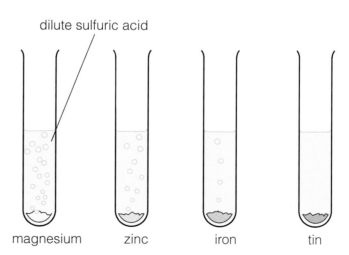

dilute sulfuric acid

magnesium   zinc   iron   tin

Some cans for food and drinks are made of steel with a coating of tin on the inside. Others are made of aluminium. Tin and aluminium both react very slowly with dilute acids, so they are safe to use for food cans.

Aluminium reacts with oxygen in the air, forming a layer of aluminium oxide. This layer protects the aluminium from corrosion by acid. This protective layer means that aluminium can be used for storing acidic food.

Testing for hydrogen

We can collect some of the gas that bubbles off when zinc reacts with acid. We do this by passing the gas along a delivery tube and up through water. Hydrogen does not dissolve in water, and it has a low density so it floats.

Once a test tube full of the gas has been collected, you can test it by putting a lighted splint near the top. Hydrogen gas is explosive, so you will hear a 'pop'! Hydrogen is the only gas that pops like this. If you have a test tube of pure hydrogen, it may burn more slowly and not give a 'pop'. The hydrogen needs some air mixed with it to burn quickly enough to 'pop'.

All acids contain hydrogen. Hydrochloric acid contains **hydro**gen and **chlor**ine and gets its name from both of these.

Acids and metal oxides

Copper does not react with dilute sulfuric acid, but black copper oxide does if you heat it. A blue solution of copper sulfate is formed. If you leave the solution to evaporate, you will see crystals of copper sulfate.

The general word equation is:

> acid + metal oxide → salt + water

The word equation for the reaction between sulfuric acid and copper oxide is:

> sulfuric acid + copper oxide → copper sulfate + water

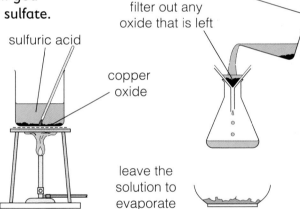

Questions

1. What are the products of the reaction between a metal and an acid?

2. Copy and complete the following word equations.
   a magnesium + sulfuric acid → _____ + hydrogen
   b zinc + hydrochloric → _____ + _____
         acid
   c _____ + _____ → iron + _____
                                          sulfate

3. Predict what would happen if you put an iron nail into a beaker of hydrochloric acid. What two products would you end up with?

4. You are given three test tubes containing samples of hydrogen, carbon dioxide and air. Plan an experiment to find out which is which.

For your notes

Some acids react with many metals, eating them away. This is called **corrosion**.

When an acid reacts with a metal, a salt and hydrogen gas are produced.

Hydrogen 'pops' with a lighted splint.

Acids react with many metal oxides, making a salt and water.

Rain again ...

Pure water is neutral, but if you test rainwater with universal indicator paper, you will find that it is slightly acidic.

Rainwater is naturally acidic because some of the carbon dioxide in the air dissolves in the rain to make a weakly acidic solution of carbonic acid:

> carbon dioxide + water → carbonic acid

Rock solid?

Over millions of years, slightly acidic rainwater has slowly dissolved away limestone rocks. Limestone is mainly made of calcium carbonate so it reacts with the acid. Holes and cracks begin to appear in the rocks, as you can see in the second photo.

a Write a general word equation for this reaction.

Other rocks such as granite do not react with rainwater, but these rocks may also contain other substances which do react. This causes the rock to break up. Eventually the rock is completely broken up into the tiny grains of **minerals** that make up **soil**. When rocks break up by reacting with rainwater we call it **chemical weathering**.

b What kind of substances in granite rocks might react with acids?

Learn about

► Acid rain

► Its effects on buildings and living things

Adding to the acidity

Whenever fossil fuels are burned, such as gas, petrol, oil and coal, the rain is made more acidic.

Fossil fuels contain small amounts of sulfur. When sulfur burns it produces sulfur dioxide, which is acidic.

> sulfur + oxygen → sulfur dioxide

Acid rain

Sulfur dioxide causes pollution. It dissolves in the rain, eventually making sulfuric acid which is corrosive. Rain containing sulfuric acid is called '**acid rain**'. Acid rain causes several environmental problems:

- Acid rain poisons fish in lakes. If the pH falls below 5.5, neither the fish nor the organisms they feed on can survive.

- Acid rain damages the leaves of trees, stopping them photosynthesising. It also damages the bark, making it easier for insects and disease-causing microorganisms to get in. The acid also washes minerals that the tree needs out of the soil, and releases poisonous aluminium which can damage plant roots.

- Acid rain dissolves away buildings and statues made of limestone or marble because they contain calcium carbonate. The Parthenon in Greece, the Sphinx in Egypt and York Minster in England are all ancient statues or buildings that are renowned for their architectural beauty. They all show signs of corrosion.

(c) What is the critical pH for the survival of fish in lakes?

(d) Which element is released in acidic soil that is toxic to plants?

Tackling the problem

Lime, which is a base, is added to some acidic lakes in Canada to neutralise them. If the rock that forms the bed of the lake is limestone, it will contain calcium carbonate. This neutralises the acid and naturally reduces the problem.

'Clean Air' laws have set limits for sulfur dioxide emission from companies and car exhausts. Tall chimneys help to take away the sulfur dioxide from coal-burning power stations, but unfortunately it finds its way to the lakes and forests of Norway and Sweden. A long-term solution is to use fossil fuels less by saving energy and sharing cars.

Questions

1. Rainwater does not burn your skin. Why not?

2. Explain how rain causes chemical weathering.

3. How does burning fossil fuels cause acid rain?

4. Describe three ways in which acid rain harms the environment.

5. Imagine you are a geologist working for a copper mining company in Canada. You have been asked to test the bedrock from a nearby lake to see if it will neutralise any acid produced by the mining works. Plan an investigation to solve the problem.

For your notes

Rainwater is always slightly acidic. It reacts with calcium carbonate in rocks causing **chemical weathering**.

Burning fossil fuels causes pollution which makes rain more acidic. This '**acid rain**' poisons fish and damages trees. It also corrodes buildings.

The answer lies in the soil

Soil acidity

James Beck is worried about the acidic soil on his farm. He has decided to use 'Super-base' to neutralise the soil. He wants to use enough base to neutralise all the acid in the soil, but not too much because that would leave the soil alkaline. It would also waste money.

Think about

► Compensation

Ask an expert

James has asked soil scientist Sarah Jones to advise him.

I will mix a sample of soil with water, and then measure the number of acid particles dissolved in the water. Then I will be able to estimate the amount of base we need.

Sarah finds that to neutralise the acid particles, James must add the same number of 'Superbase' particles. The diagram on the right shows this.

Sarah calculates that one bag of base dissolved in 10 litres of water will neutralise the soil in the field.

ⓐ How reliable do you think Sarah's calculation is?

James is still keen to save money. He decides to add 10 litres of water to Sarah's solution. He uses 10 litres of it now and saves the other half for next time.

ⓑ Do you think this will make any difference to the amount of soil he can neutralise?

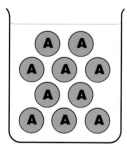

acid particles in the soil

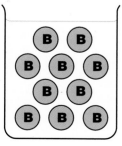

same number of base particles needed to neutralise acid particles

not to scale

chloroplasts

root hair

stoma

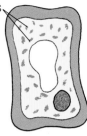
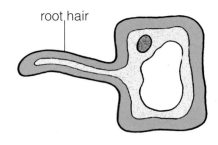

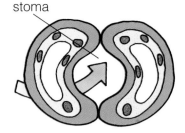

Palisade cells in plant leaves have lots of chloroplasts closely packed near the top of the cell so they absorb as much light energy as possible for photosynthesis.

Root hair cells are in the roots of plants. The root hair is a long finger-like part of the cell. This adaptation gives a very large surface area so the cell absorbs as much water as possible.

Red blood cells are part of your blood. They are adapted to carry oxygen for respiration. They have no nucleus and are flexible so they pass easily through small blood vessels.

Two **guard cells** make up a **stoma**, the hole in the underside of a leaf which lets gases in and out. Each cell is a half-circle so they fit together in pairs to make a stoma.

Tissues

In big organisms, there are groups of cells performing one function. We call a group of cells like this a **tissue**. An example is muscle tissue. This is made up of many muscle cells all working together to move parts of your body. An individual cell can only make a tiny movement so it takes thousands of cells moving together to move your arm or leg.

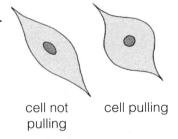

cell not
pulling

cell pulling

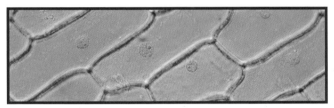

Plants also have tissues. For example, in onion skin lots of cells fit together to make a protective layer.

b Draw a diagram of several muscle cells fitting together in a tissue when they are pulling and when they are not pulling.

c Describe an adaptation of an onion skin cell that helps it make a skin tissue.

Questions

1. Make a table with three headings: 'Cell', 'Function', 'Adaptations'. Fill it in for each type of cell listed in the text above.

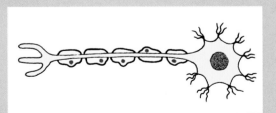

2. The picture opposite shows a nerve cell. Describe how it is adapted to its function.

3. Explain what a tissue is.

4. Explain what life processes go on in simple organisms, and where they happen.

5. Why do multicellular organisms need specialised cells?

6. For **a–d**, explain what life processes it is involved with.
   a egg cell   **b** palisade cell   **c** sperm cell   **d** red blood cell

For your notes

Many cells are **specialised**.

Cells are adapted to their special **functions**.

A group of cells working together is called a **tissue**.

21

Tissues working together

In plants and animals, different types of tissue are grouped together so that they in turn can work together.

The function of your heart is to pump blood around the body. However, many different individual processes help with this. To perform these many processes the heart is made up of several different tissues.

- The lining of the heart is made of a tissue which is a bit like epithelial tissue. It allows a smooth flow of blood.

- The walls of the heart contain muscle tissue. These walls squeeze and force blood out of the heart.

- Inside the heart are valves that only let the blood flow in one direction.

- String-like tissues stop the valves turning inside out.

A group of tissues working together form an **organ**. Your heart is an example of an organ.

ⓐ Why are the walls of the heart made of muscle?

ⓑ What would happen if the heart did not have valves?

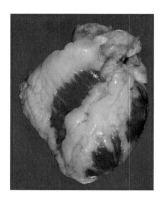

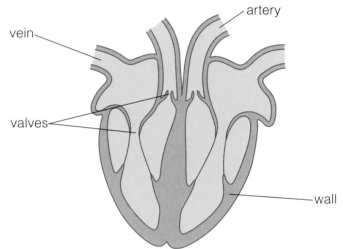

artery
vein
valves
wall

lungs

heart

body

The circulatory system

The heart does not work alone. To do its job properly, it has to work with other cells, tissues and organs. A group of organs working together is called an **organ system**. The heart is part of an organ system called the **circulatory system**.

The blood in the circulatory system transports oxygen from the lungs to all the cells in the body. Oxygen is needed for **respiration**. The red blood cells carry the oxygen. The waste product of respiration is carbon dioxide. This is transported back to the lungs where it is removed from the body.

Blood is transported around the body in tubes called **blood vessels**. The inside of the blood vessels is lined with smooth tissue.

There are different types of blood vessel:

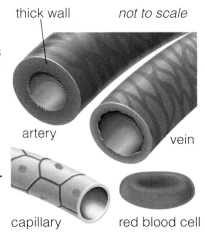

thick wall　　*not to scale*

- **Arteries** carry blood away from the heart. Arteries have very thick walls made from muscle tissue.
- **Veins** carry blood back towards the heart. Veins have valves inside them that allow the blood to flow in one direction only. Without valves, gravity would pull all the blood down into your feet!
- **Capillaries** are tiny blood vessels that carry the blood deep into organs and tissues. The walls of a capillary are made of just a single layer of cells. This allows oxygen and carbon dioxide to pass through easily for respiration.

artery　　　　　　　　vein

capillary　　　red blood cell

c Why do you think the walls of arteries need to be thick and strong?

Other organ systems

The human body is made up of lots of different organ systems. The male and female **reproductive systems** allow us to reproduce. The **digestive system** breaks down food, the **respiratory system** takes in oxygen and gets rid of carbon dioxide, and the **nervous system** controls the body. All of these organ systems work together to make up an organism.

cell
(heart muscle cell)

organism
(human)

tissue
(heart muscle)

organ
(heart)

organ system
(circulatory system)

Like animals, plants also have organs. Each organ is made of different tissues. Some plant organs are described below.

- **Leaves** collect light energy and allow gases in and out for photosynthesis.
- **Petals** guide insects to the flower to help in reproduction.
- The **stem** holds the plant upright and transports water and minerals up from the roots. It also transports food around the plant.
- The **root** takes in water and minerals from the soil. It also anchors the plant firmly in the ground.

Plants also have organ systems. **Flowers** are the reproductive organ systems.

petal

leaf

stem

root

Questions

1. Explain the difference between an organ and a tissue.

2. What is an organ system?

3. Explain the function of each of these systems:
   a circulatory system　　b respiratory system
   c nervous system　　　　d digestive system.

4. List four organs of a plant. For each organ, explain which of the seven life processes it is adapted to carry out.

5. Describe the journey of a red blood cell around the body, starting and finishing at the heart.

For your notes

An **organ** is a group of tissues working together.

A group of organs working together is called an **organ system**.

Bones and joints

The skeletal system

You have seen that the circulatory system transports substances around the body. Another important organ system in your body is the **skeletal system**, or **skeleton**. This is made up of all the bones in your body. The skeleton has three main functions:

- It protects important organs like the brain, lungs and heart.
- It supports the body and lets us stand upright.
- It allows us to move.

Bone is a strong, rigid but lightweight tissue. It is made mainly of calcium salts. The calcium makes the bones strong and hard. Most bones are hollow which makes them light.

In the bone are living cells, so bones have arteries and veins to carry blood to and from the bone cells.

ⓐ Why is it important for bones to be light?

ⓑ Why do bones need a blood supply?

Moving bones

Look at the tip of your finger. Wiggle it about a bit. Look at the way that it moves.

Now look at your whole arm. Move it around from the shoulder. Does it move in the same way as your finger?

ⓒ Describe the differences between the way your finger moves and the way your arm moves.

At particular points in your skeleton there are **joints**. Joints allow the bones to move. There are different types of joint, and each type allows bones to move in a different way. The joints in your knuckles are different from the joints in your shoulders. Three different types of joint are shown below.

ⓓ What would your body be like if you didn't have joints?

Learn about

► Bones
► Joints

Did you know?

A newborn baby has 350 bones, but a fully grown adult has only 206. Small bones join together as you grow up.

- **Hinge joint:** bones can move only backwards and forwards, as in the knuckle and the knee.

- **Ball and socket joint:** bones can move in all directions, as in the shoulder and hip.

- **Pivot joint:** allows some circular movement, as in the neck.

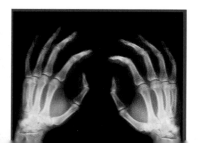
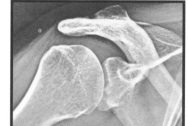
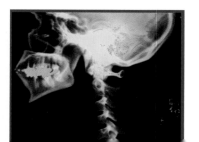

Holding it all together

The diagram shows the structure of the knee joint. At a joint, the bones are held together by **ligaments**. Ligaments stop your skeleton falling apart. They are made from a very strong stringy tissue that does not stretch very much.

At the ends of each bone is a very tough, smooth tissue called **cartilage**. This reduces friction and helps the ends of the bones to slide over each other as they move. In between the two bones is a liquid called **synovial fluid**. This helps to reduce friction and also absorbs shock. Cartilage and synovial fluid act as lubricants.

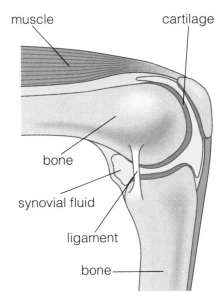

e Explain why cartilage and synovial fluid are important. What would happen if we did not have them in our joints?

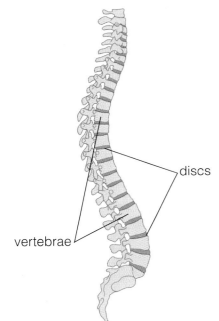

When joints go wrong

Cartilage can occasionally tear during exercise. This can be very painful and an operation is needed to remove any loose cartilage inside the joint.

Humans are vertebrates, which means we have a backbone made up of lots of bones called **vertebrae**. In between are tiny discs of cartilage. Sometimes one of these discs may 'pop' out of place. We call this injury a slipped disc.

The hand in the photo is affected by **arthritis**. The joints become very swollen and painful as the bones rub together. Sometimes the bones in the joints may join together or move out of place. There are many different causes of arthritis, including infection and old age. The most severe type of arthritis is called rheumatoid arthritis.

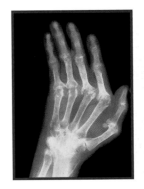

Some types of arthritis can be cured by replacing the joint with an artificial one.

Questions

1. Describe the functions of the skeletal system.

2. Give three properties of bone that make it suitable for its function.

3. Make a table with three headings: 'Type of joint', 'Example' and 'The way it moves'. Complete the table for the three types of joint.

4. Rebecca was trying to lift a heavy box when she got a bad pain in her back. The doctor said she had slipped a disc. Explain to her what this means.

5. Give three properties that are important for materials used to make artificial joints and explain why you chose them.

For your notes

The **skeletal system** is made of over 200 bones.

These bones can be moved at joints and are held together by **ligaments**.

The three main types of joint are **hinge**, **ball and socket** and **pivot**.

Joints contain **cartilage** and **synovial fluid** to reduce friction.

The muscular system

Bones cannot move by themselves.
To move them you need **muscles**.

A muscle is an organ made of muscle tissue, along with other tissues such as capillaries to supply the muscle with blood. Muscle tissue is made from muscle cells. These cells are long and thin. They are arranged in bundles called **muscle fibres**. These fibres are also arranged in long bundles. If you look closely at muscle you can see that is made up from long thin fibres.

Muscles are joined onto bones by special fibres called **tendons**.
Tendons do not stretch at all.

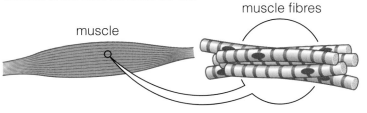

muscle

muscle fibres

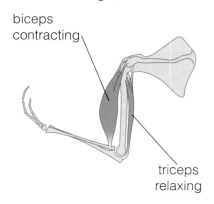

Working in pairs

Muscle cells are long and thin, but they are able to get shorter and fatter. This is called **contracting**. When all of the muscle cells in the muscle contract at the same time, the muscle can make a bone move. When the muscle cells become long and thin again, we say the muscle is **relaxing**.

A muscle can pull on a bone to move it, but cannot push it back. Muscles work in pairs to move bones one way and then back again. One muscle contracts to pull the bone one way, then it relaxes while the other muscle contracts to pull the bone back. We call this pair of muscles working together an **antagonistic pair**.

raising the arm

biceps contracting

triceps relaxing

a Look at the weightlifter below, and the diagrams opposite.
  i Which muscles contract to pull his arms up and lift the weights?
  ii Which muscles contract to let him put the weights down again?

lowering the arm

biceps relaxing

triceps contracting

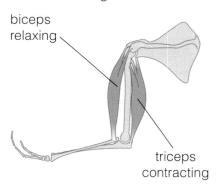

When the weightlifter holds the weights still, both sets of muscles are contracting. The biceps is pulling upwards and the triceps is pulling against it to keep the arm in one place. When two muscles are both pulling with the same force we say they are in **equilibrium**.

Lasting the distance

Using your muscles regularly when you exercise makes them stronger and able to work for longer. Compare the different runners in the photos.

Start of the 100m sprint. *The London Marathon.*

The sprinter has built up large muscles that are very powerful so that she can run very fast for a short period of time. These muscles get tired quite quickly. The marathon runner's muscles do not need to be so powerful. They need to keep working for a long time without getting tired.

Each athlete exercises in a special way to train her muscles for her kind of race. The sprinter will spend a lot of time in the gym lifting weights. The fibres inside her muscles get bigger and thicker. This means that her muscles will get bigger and more powerful.

The marathon runner will spend a lot of time running, cycling and swimming. This type of exercise will increase the number of capillaries inside the muscles and make the muscles more efficient. It will not make the muscles much bigger.

b Why will having more capillaries in the muscle be good for a marathon runner?

Different muscles for different functions

There are three different types of muscle in your body. The first type is the muscle that makes your body move. You can control these muscles, so they are called voluntary muscles.

A second type of muscle is controlled automatically by your body without you thinking about it. An example is the muscle that moves food through your gut. This type of muscle is called involuntary muscle.

The third type of muscle is only found in the heart. This special muscle keeps on working without getting tired.

c Explain why it is important that the muscle in your heart does not get tired.

Questions

1. What is the difference between a ligament and a tendon?

2. Describe how an antagonistic pair of muscles works.

3. Explain why a champion 100-metre runner would not be so good at running a marathon.

4. Roger wants to run the London Marathon next year. Produce an exercise plan for Roger to get him ready for the event. Apart from exercise, what else should Roger do?

5. Is each of the following changes brought about by voluntary muscle or involuntary muscle?
   a Your tummy rumbles when you are hungry.
   b The hole in the front of your eye (the pupil) gets bigger when it goes dark.
   c You get up and turn the heating on when you get cold.

Did you know?

The largest muscle in your body is your bottom. Its name is the gluteus maximus.

For your notes

Muscles are made of muscle tissue. They can **contract** and **relax**.

Bones move when a muscle contracts.

Muscles can only pull, they cannot push, so they work in **antagonistic pairs**.

Examining Tharg

Tharg, the alien?

It's the year 2516 and the latest space probe has brought back an organism from a distant galaxy. The astronauts called the organism Tharg. A group of biologists are examining Tharg to find out what kind of organism he is, and whether his family might originally have come from Earth. They make measurements to collect a lot of data about him, so they can analyse it.

The body map

You have the job of drawing a scale diagram of Tharg's body to fit on an A4 piece of paper. Your colleagues have given you the measurements they have taken.

To fit a drawing of Tharg on the paper you will have to use a **ratio** of **1:5**. A ratio is another way of giving a scale factor. For example, if you are measuring in centimetres, a ratio of 1:5 tells you that '1 centimetre on the scale diagram represents 5 centimetres in real life'. You say that the ratio of the scale diagram to real life is 'one to five'. You have to specify whether you are giving the ratio of the drawing to real life or real life to the drawing, so that you know which number in the ratio applies to which measurement. This ratio means Tharg is 5 times bigger than the scale diagram.

(a) Will you be scaling up or scaling down?

(b) Calculate the measurements for the scale diagram from the real-life measurements below, so that the ratio of the scale diagram to real-life Tharg is 1:5.

Height	Arm length	Leg length	Foot length	Hand length
92 cm	30 cm	35 cm	27 cm	5 cm

When you scale something up or down, there is a relationship between the real size and the size you draw it. In a scale diagram, all the parts are scaled up or down by the same amount.

(c) If Tharg's index finger was 0.5 cm long on your scale diagram, how long would his finger really be?

Simple ratios

You can see that a ratio has the number 1 on one side. If you know the length of Tharg's foot is 24 cm, and you decide to draw it 6 cm long, you can say that the ratio of Tharg's foot to the drawing is 24:6. It is easier to do calculations if you always give ratios in the form 1:? or ?:1, so that there is always a 1 in the ratio. To do this, you simplify the ratio by dividing both numbers by the smallest number.

24:6

divide by 6 = 4:1

One of the biologists did a scan of Tharg to get an image of his heart. She also drew a large scale diagram of it, but has forgotten what ratio she used to draw it. Her boss wants her to add the ratio to her diagram.

d The width of the heart on the scan was 8 cm, and the width on the drawing is 24 cm. What was the ratio of the heart on the scan to the drawing?

e Why do you think she drew a scale diagram?

Next, your colleagues want to study Tharg's size in relation to the average human being. They give you the data for Tharg and for the average human. They want you to calculate the ratio of Tharg to the human for each measurement.

f Copy the table and complete it.

g What do the ratios show about the size of Tharg in comparison to humans?

	Height	Arm length	Leg length	Foot length	Hand length
Tharg	92 cm	30 cm	35 cm	27 cm	5 cm
Human	184 cm	60 cm	105 cm	27 cm	20 cm
Ratio T:H					

The blood count

Finally, the team wanted to find out how many green blood cells Tharg has in his body. Obviously they could not drain all his blood and count the cells one by one! Instead they took a small amount of blood, or a **sample**, and found out how many blood cells there are in that. We call this **sampling**.

In 1 cm^3 of Tharg's blood there are 25 green blood cells. Now you can scale up to find out how many blood cells there are in 10 cm^3 of blood.

The ratio of 'the volume you know about' to 'the volume you want to find out about' is: $1\,cm^3 : 10\,cm^3$

h What do you need to scale up by?

i How many green blood cells are there in 10 cm^3?

j How many green blood cells are there in 100 cm^3?

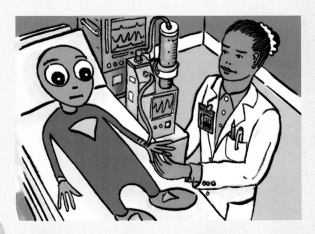

Because Tharg is a super-intelligent being, he actually knows how many litres of blood his body contains. He tells you he has 3.5 litres of blood. There are 1000 cm^3 in 1 litre.

k How many green blood cells does he have altogether? Explain how you got this answer.

Questions

1. 1 cm^3 of Tharg's blood also contains 9 pink blood cells. How many pink blood cells are there in his body? Explain how you got this answer.

2. Why do you think it is important to describe the relationship between two things carefully before you give the ratio between them, in order to decide whether you are scaling up or scaling down?

3. Suggest how a builder, a pharmacist and an interior designer might find it useful to use ratios.

One small step for man

Getting to know the Earth

For thousands of years people believed that the Earth was flat and it was surrounded by water. They thought that if a boat sailed too far away from land, it would fall off the edge of the world.

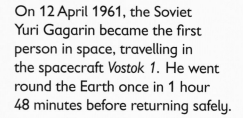

Aristotle (384–325 BC) first proved that the Earth was a sphere. Later, in 270 BC, Eratosthenes gave a very good estimate of the size of the Earth. It was another 2000 years before a man could look down from space and see with his own eyes that the Earth is really a sphere.

The race into space

The first powered aircraft flew across the English Channel between England and France in 1909. As technology developed after the Second World War, the space race between the USA and the Soviet Union began. The first object to be sent into orbit around the Earth was called *Sputnik 1*, shown in the photo on the right. It was launched by the Soviet Union on 4 October 1957. It stayed in space for 52 days. *Sputnik 2* was launched on 3 November 1957 along with the first living thing to travel in space, a Russian dog called Laika. It stayed in space for 162 days.

a Why do you think a dog was used instead of a human in *Sputnik 2*?

On 12 April 1961, the Soviet Yuri Gagarin became the first person in space, travelling in the spacecraft *Vostok 1*. He went round the Earth once in 1 hour 48 minutes before returning safely.

The first American in space was Alan Shepard, who spent 15 minutes there. John Glenn was the first American to orbit the Earth. He went round three times on 20 February 1962. His flight lasted almost 5 hours.

The first woman in space was a Russian. Valentina Tereshkova was the pilot of *Vostok 6*. On 16 June 1963 she went around the Earth 48 times.

From the Earth to the Moon

The rivalry between the USA and the Soviet Union continued. In May 1961 the American president John F. Kennedy planned to get an American on the Moon before 1970. The Americans started work to design and test the technology needed to get people on the Moon.

On 20 July 1969 *Apollo 11* made its successful journey to the Moon. While astronaut Michael Collins stayed to pilot the command module above the Moon, Neil Armstrong and Edwin (Buzz) Aldrin took the lunar module down to the Moon's surface. The landing was watched live by millions of people on television. Neil Armstrong's first words on the Moon were: 'That's one small step for man, one giant leap for mankind.'

b What do you think Neil Armstrong meant by this?

What is out there?

In order to investigate our Solar System further, scientists have used space probes controlled by robots. In 1962, *Mariner 2* became the first successful probe to go to a planet when it flew past Venus. In 1976, probes *Viking 1* and *Viking 2* landed robots on Mars. They were able to send back thousands of photographs of Mars and study its environment. More recently the Mars *Pathfinder* probe sent amazing pictures of the surface of Mars, such as the one shown here.

In 1986, another probe called *Giotto* was used to study Halley's Comet. The probe was able to go into the head of the comet and send pictures of its icy core.

c Why do you think it has been necessary to use robots to study the Solar System further?

What's next?

The quest continues to explore our Solar System and beyond.

- There are plans to build a spaceship that could take people to Mars. This would be very difficult, since it would take nearly a year to get there and another year to get back.
- NASA is looking at new ways to make space travel easier and cheaper. The X-33 can be launched from a jumbo jet and can land on a normal runway.
- The recent discovery of ice on the Moon means that it might be possible to maintain life on the Moon.

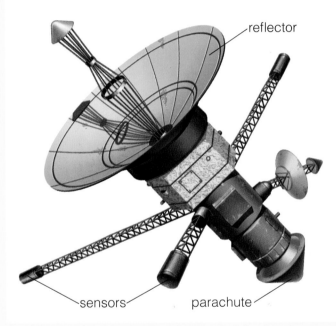

A space probe.

Questions

1. Why do you think people first thought the Earth was flat?

2. a What problems would you have if you were a weightless astronaut in space?
   b What forces would be exerted on you?

3. What could astronauts use the ice on the Moon for? Why might this be helpful?

4. One of the problems of sending probes into space is the expense. First they have to be developed and launched from rockets, and at the end of their journey they usually crash-land or disappear into space for ever. If you were a space scientist, how would you tackle these problems?

5. Imagine you are the first person on the Moon. Write what you would say to the millions of people watching about being on the Moon and seeing the Earth from there.

Round the Sun

Learn about

➤ Our Solar System

Orbiting the Sun

The Earth goes round the Sun once every year.
The path it takes is called an **orbit**. Our **Solar System** is made up of the Sun along with nine planets, including the Earth, orbiting the Sun. The Solar System also contains **asteroids**, **comets**, **meteors** and **meteorites** which are made of ice, rock, dust and gas. They are much smaller than planets, measuring less than 1000 km across. The asteroids are mostly rocky objects found in the **asteroid belt** between Mars and Jupiter.

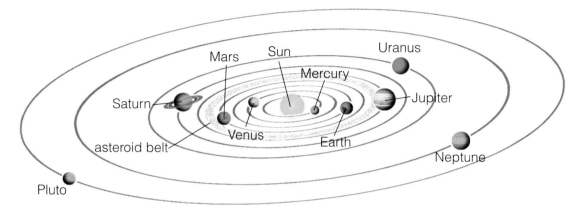

Mars · Sun · Uranus · Mercury · Saturn · Jupiter · asteroid belt · Venus · Earth · Neptune · Pluto

a What does the name 'Solar System' describe? Why is it a good name?

Planetary facts

Mercury is a small rocky planet that is closest to the Sun. It has no atmosphere and is very hot, up to 427 °C.

Venus is the hottest planet, about 480 °C. It is rocky with an atmosphere of carbon dioxide.

Earth is a rocky planet with an average temperature of 22 °C. It has water and an atmosphere of nitrogen and oxygen. It is the only planet we know about with living organisms.

Mars is a red, rocky, cold planet (−23 °C) with an atmosphere of carbon dioxide.

Jupiter is a giant planet made mainly of liquids and gases. The temperature there is about −150 °C. Jupiter is famous for its Great Red Spot which is probably due to a giant storm. It has many moons.

Saturn is a cold (−180 °C) giant planet made mainly from gases. It has beautiful rings of ice particles around it and many moons.

Uranus is a pale green gas giant that has 15 moons and a number of rings like Saturn. The temperature is –210 °C.

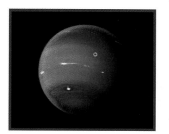

Neptune is a bluish gas giant with a cold atmosphere (–220 °C). It has the strongest winds on any planet.

Pluto is rocky. It is the smallest planet and is furthest from the Sun. The temperature is –230 °C. Some people are not sure whether it is a planet at all because it is so small and has an irregular orbit.

b Suggest why it seems the Earth is the only planet suitable for life.

Differences between the planets

As you can see, the conditions on each planet are very different. Their sizes also vary. Five of them are drawn to scale here.

Mercury 7 mm   Venus 18 mm   Earth 19 mm   Mars 10 mm   Pluto 3 mm

c Why are the four planets Jupiter, Saturn, Uranus and Neptune not drawn on the page here?

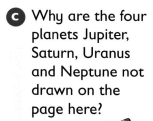

Planet	Diameter to same scale as drawings
Jupiter	210 mm
Saturn	178 mm
Uranus	76 mm
Neptune	75 mm

How long is a year?

A **day** is the 24 hours taken for the Earth to spin once on its axis. We call a **year** ($365\frac{1}{4}$ Earth days) the time it takes for the Earth to orbit the Sun. Mercury is closest to the Sun and takes only 88 Earth days to orbit the Sun. Pluto is the furthest from the Sun and takes 248 Earth years to orbit the Sun.

Questions

1. Make up a rhyme to remind you of the planets of the Solar System in order.

2. We can see six planets with the naked eye. Which do you think they are?

3. Look at what the nine planets are made from. Can you divide them into groups? Explain your answer.

4. How many times longer does Pluto take to orbit the Sun than Mercury?

5. Discuss what would happen if the Earth was further away from the Sun.

6. **a** What is the relationship between a planet's distance from the Sun and its temperature?
   b Can you explain this relationship?

For your notes

The **Solar System** is made up of the Sun and the nine planets along with their moons and other objects such as **comets, meteors** and **asteroids**.

The planets differ from each other in many ways such as diameter, distance from the Sun, what they are made of and the conditions there.

Shedding light on things

Seeing the light

Look at the photos. All these objects produce light.

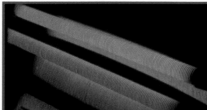

a Explain how we are able to see these things.

Light travels in a straight line, at a speed of 300 000 000 m/s. It is sometimes difficult to understand just how fast light is. If you have ever been to America you will know that it takes a long time to fly there. Even if you flew on Concorde, it would take 3 hours to fly to New York from London. Light is so fast that it gets there in a fraction of a second. In fact, it can travel from London to New York and back again more than 25 times in one second!

The Sun as a star

Our Sun is a source of light for everyone on Earth. It is a star, and all stars are sources of light. It takes just 8.3 minutes for the light from the Sun to reach us.

b Most of the space between the Sun and the Earth is empty space (a vacuum). Explain why the light is able to reach us but sound isn't able to.

c How many times further is it from the Earth to the Sun than from London to New York?

The photo opposite shows some stars in the night sky. When you look up at the stars, it's hard to believe that each one is a sun. Apart from our Sun, the nearest star is Alpha Centauri which is about 40 000 billion km (40 000 000 000 000 km) away.

Like all stars, the Sun is a huge ball of very hot gas. The surface temperature of the Sun is 5700 °C. It is made of 71% hydrogen with 21% helium and very small amounts of other elements.

Did you know?

The light from Alpha Centauri takes 4.3 years to reach us. This means that we see Alpha Centauri as it looked 4.3 years ago. We are looking backwards through time! If the star disappeared, we wouldn't notice it wasn't there for 4.3 years.

Did you know?

The centre of the Sun has a temperature of 15 000 000 °C.

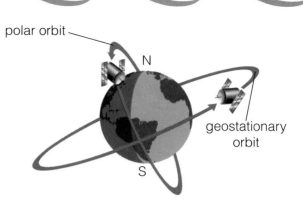

polar orbit

N

geostationary orbit

S

Geostationary and polar orbits

Artificial satellites are put into different orbits depending on the job they are going to do. Some orbit the Earth at the same speed as the Earth is turning on its axis. These are called **geostationary satellites**. Geostationary satellites orbit the Earth once every 24 hours, which means they stay in the same place over the Earth's surface. Other satellites are in orbits that take them over the North and South Poles. These are called **polar orbits**.

Uses of artificial satellites

Artificial satellites are useful to us in many ways:

1. **Communication satellites** send radio, TV and telephone messages around the world. These are geostationary satellites.

2. **Exploration satellites** carry telescopes and can take clear pictures of planets. They can also look at the universe. The Hubble telescope is a good example.

3. **Military satellites** are used for spying on other countries.

4. **Weather satellites** take pictures of cloud formations and send them to Earth to be analysed. This helps the weather forecasters to predict our weather.

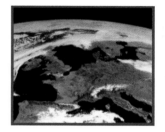

5. **Navigation satellites** are used by ships, cars and planes to find their position on the Earth. They can give the position to within 10 metres.

6. **Observation satellites** take detailed photos of the Earth. They can show volcanic eruptions, floods and oil spills.

Questions

1. **a** What is a gravitational force?
   b What does the strength of the gravitational force between two objects depend on?

2. Describe how the effect of the Earth's gravitational force on a spaceship will change on a voyage from Earth to the Moon. Explain how this change will affect the mass and weight of the astronaut during the trip.

3. What is the advantage of a satellite that is in:
   a a geostationary orbit?
   b a polar orbit?

4. People are launching more and more probes, satellites and craft into space. Why could this cause problems in the future?

5. The Russians planned to use a giant mirror in space to reflect light from the Sun onto a city at night.
   a What are the advantages and disadvantages of this idea?
   b Draw a diagram to show how this would work.

6. Prepare a presentation for the rest of your class about the importance of satellites to us.

For your notes

A **satellite** is an object that orbits a larger object.

The planets are held in orbit around the Sun by the **gravitational force** of the Sun.

There are natural satellites such as the Earth and planets orbiting the Sun, and the Moon orbiting the Earth.

Artificial satellites are machines launched into space by people. They are used for communicating across our planet or studying space.

Making models

The Solar System

Class 8J were studying the Solar System. They were drawing diagrams and making models that represented the Solar System. Some of the information they used is shown in the table. The Sun is 1 392 000 km in diameter.

Planet	Diameter (to nearest 1000 km)	Average distance from Sun (to nearest 1 000 000 km)	Furthest planet gets from Sun (to nearest 1 000 000 km)	Closest planet gets to Sun (to nearest 1 000 000 km)	Tilt of orbit (to nearest degree)
Mercury	5000	58 000 000	70 000 000	46 000 000	7
Venus	12 000	108 000 000	109 000 000	107 000 000	3
Earth	13 000	150 000 000	152 000 000	147 000 000	0
Mars	7000	228 000 000	249 000 000	207 000 000	2
Jupiter	143 000	780 000 000	816 000 000	741 000 000	1
Saturn	121 000	1 427 000 000	1 507 000 000	1 347 000 000	2
Uranus	51 000	2 871 000 000	3 004 000 000	2 735 000 000	1
Neptune	50 000	4 504 000 000	4 537 000 000	4 456 000 000	2
Pluto	2000	5 900 000 000	7 375 000 000	4 425 000 000	17

Relative sizes

Ian, Karl and Darren decided to make a model showing the sizes of the planets. Darren brought in a yellow beach ball to be the Sun. Karl and Ian brought in other balls to represent the planets.

a Karl also brought in a rugby ball. Why did they decide not to use the rugby ball?

b Decide which ball should stand for each planet.

Ian, Karl and Darren presented their model to the rest of the class. They said that their model shows the relative sizes of the Sun and the planets. The class **evaluated** the model. First, they said the good things about the model.

The balls are spheres, like the Sun and the planets.

Uranus and Neptune are almost the same size, and the netball and the volleyball are almost the same size.

Ball	Diameter in cm
Beach	40
Basketball	23.9
Football	22.3
Netball	21.3
Volleyball	20.7
Cricket	7.3
Tennis	6.4
Squash	4.4
Golf	4.3
Table tennis	3.8
Marble	1.5

c Suggest four other ways in which this model represents the Sun and the planets.

We can also draw a circle to represent each atom in the molecules, as shown opposite.

Carbon dioxide, nitrogen dioxide, methane and glucose are more examples of compounds that are made up of molecules.

Carbon dioxide and nitrogen dioxide are gases present in air in small amounts. Carbon dioxide is produced by combustion and respiration reactions. Nitrogen dioxide is a pollutant formed in car engines.

hydrogen   oxygen   water

carbon dioxide   nitrogen dioxide

(a) Nitrogen molecules contain two nitrogen atoms. Use circles to show the atoms in a molecule of:
   i nitrogen   **ii** oxygen   **iii** nitrogen dioxide.

Chemistry's code

Instead of using circles to represent atoms in molecules, we can use just the symbol that represents the element. Glucose is an example of a more complex molecule. Imagine drawing all these circles!

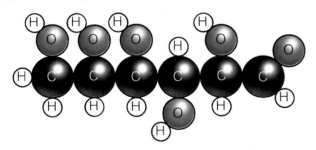

You can see that it is much easier to write letters to represent a glucose molecule than it is to draw a collection of circles.

The 6 shows there are 6 carbon atoms.

The 6 shows there are 6 oxygen atoms.

$$C_6H_{12}O_6$$

The 12 shows there are 12 hydrogen atoms.

For water, to represent the two hydrogen atoms we write an H and use the number 2 after it, slightly smaller and below the letter. So we represent a molecule of water as H_2O or a molecule of carbon dioxide as CO_2. This is the **formula** of the compound.

(b) Use formulae to write equations for producing:
   i water from hydrogen and oxygen
   ii carbon dioxide from carbon and oxygen.

Questions

1. Chlorine reacts with hydrogen to form hydrogen chloride gas.
   a Write a word equation for this reaction showing the molecules.
   b Beneath the word equation, write the formula equation for this reaction.

2. Methane has the formula CH_4.
   a Draw a methane molecule.
   b What is the ratio of the different atoms in the molecule?

3. **a** Write down the formulae for a carbon atom and an oxygen molecule forming a carbon dioxide molecule.
   b What are the ratios of different atoms in the carbon dioxide molecule?

For your notes

There are about 100 elements that are combined in different ways to make all the materials we have.

Different types of atom are joined together to make compounds.

A molecule is a group of atoms joined together.

Elements, compounds and molecules can be represented by **formulae**.

All change!

Melting and freezing

The diagram shows a temperature probe in a test tube of ice. The computer will draw a graph of the temperature of the ice against time. The diagram on the right shows the graph that you might see.

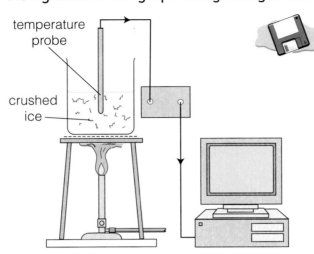

At the beginning, the ice is a solid. The molecules are close together in an orderly **lattice arrangement**. The molecules are vibrating slightly. There are tiny **forces of attraction** between the molecules, which hold them together. Energy from the flame gives the molecules in the ice more energy, which makes them vibrate faster. As they vibrate faster, the temperature of the ice rises, as shown on the graph (**P**).

When the temperature of the ice reaches 0°C, something special happens. Energy from the flame makes the molecules begin to vibrate so much that they move apart from each other and move more freely. This overcomes some of the tiny forces of attraction between the molecules, and the structure of the solid begins to break down. The solid is starting to turn into a liquid. The molecules are still held together by some forces of attraction.

The temperature of the mixture of ice and water stays at 0°C, the melting point, until all the ice turns into water (**Q**). The energy from the flame is still being used to overcome some of the forces of attraction. This is a **change of physical state** from a solid to a liquid. Then the temperature will start to rise again (**R**) as energy makes the molecules move even faster.

- Changes of state
- Energy
- Temperature

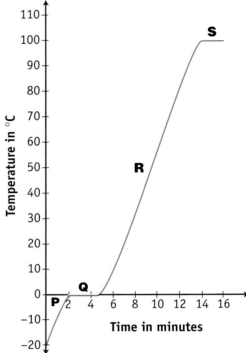

It is possible to carry out the reverse of this experiment and see what happens as water is cooled down to the melting point. The same amount of energy is given out during freezing as is taken in during melting.

(a) Sketch the graph you would expect to get if you cooled water down to melting point.

(b) Write a description of what happens to the molecules as water is cooled down to melting point.

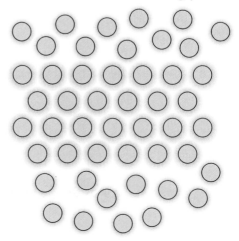

Different directions

Water melts at 0°C. It also freezes at 0°C. This is a reversible process.

> giving the molecules energy = melting
> taking energy away from the molecules = freezing

Boiling

In liquid water, there are still some forces of attraction between the molecules. As you heat water, the energy makes the molecules roll around each other faster and faster. At 100°C another change happens. The molecules are moving so fast that the tiny forces of attraction between them are completely overcome. The molecules become free to fly around all over the place. The liquid becomes a gas called steam. The temperature stays at 100°C until all the liquid becomes gas (**S**). This temperature is the boiling point. Boiling is a change of physical state from a liquid to a gas.

Condensing

Condensing is the opposite of boiling. Gas cools down and becomes a liquid.

c Use your knowledge of molecules to explain the process of condensation. You should use these words:

energy   molecules   forces of attraction

Evaporation

In a liquid, the molecules are all moving around at different speeds. Without being heated, molecules occasionally gain enough energy to break out of the surface away from the others and leave the liquid behind. Some of the liquid has evaporated – it has turned into a gas.

Evaporation only happens at the surface of the liquid where the very energetic molecules are able to escape. Boiling happens throughout the liquid. Gas is being produced inside the liquid, forming bubbles.

d Use the diagrams below to explain why hot liquids evaporate quicker than cold ones.

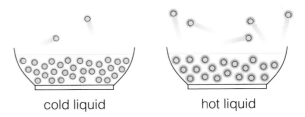

cold liquid   hot liquid

Questions

1. Explain how 0°C can be both the melting point and the freezing point of water.

2. Sulfur melts at 119°C. Compare the forces of attraction between the sulfur molecules in sulfur with the forces of attraction between the water molecules in ice.

3. Explain the difference between boiling and evaporation.

4. Look at the graph on the opposite page and answer these questions.
   a By how much did the temperature rise during the 16 minutes?
   b Explain what is happening to the molecules at each of the points **P**, **Q**, **R** and **S**.
   c For how long was the ice melting?

For your notes

Ice melts when the molecules are given enough energy to overcome the **forces of attraction** between them.

Water freezes when the molecules lose energy and become joined by strong forces of attraction.

Water boils when the molecules have enough energy to overcome the forces of attraction between them.

Condensing is the opposite of boiling. Gas molecules lose energy and gas becomes liquid.

Evaporation only happens at the surface of a liquid.

Wandering particles

What's that smell?

This perfume has a lovely scent.

This onion is making my eyes water!

This air freshener makes the whole room smell nice.

All of the things in the photos give off smells. Quite often you can smell something even when you are not near it. You would be able to smell the air freshener all over the room. It gives off a gas. Gases are made of particles which move and spread out to fill all of the space available.

You cannot see what is making the smell in the air. The smell is caused by tiny particles that are too small to see. Special cells in your nose detect these particles. Particles from an onion can even get into your eyes and make them water.

Diffusion

If someone let off a stink bomb in a corner, people sitting near it would be the first to smell it. Gradually people further and further away would smell it. Eventually everybody would notice the smell.

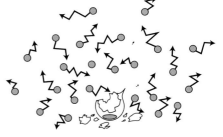

stink bomb

The stink bomb contains a bad-smelling liquid. When you let the stink bomb off, this liquid evaporates and becomes a gas. The smelly gas particles mix with particles in the air. Particles of a gas move very quickly in all directions. The smelly particles keep moving at random and eventually spread through the room.

This movement is called **diffusion**. It happens by itself, you don't need to mix or stir the substances.

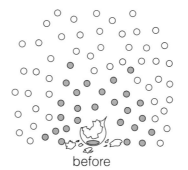

before

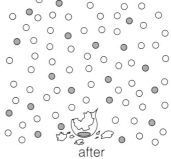

after

(a) Why would a person sitting near the stink bomb smell it before someone sitting further away?

(b) Why would the smell be stronger nearer to the stink bomb than further away?

These planes are making coloured smoke trails in the sky. After a couple of minutes the trails spread out and get fainter as the smoke particles diffuse in all directions and mix with the air particles. As the smoke particles move further apart, the trails will eventually disappear.

c Draw a diagram to show the particles in the smoke trail 1 minute, 5 minutes and 10 minutes after the display.

d Why will the trails disappear faster on a windy day?

Diffusion in liquids

Diffusion doesn't only happen in gases. The photos show diffusion happening in a liquid. Particles in a liquid are able to move about a little, but not as much as in a gas. You can see the purple colour spread out as the particles gradually move and mix into the water.

e Why was the purple colour at the top of the beaker stronger at 6 o'clock than it was at 12 o'clock?

Hot and cold

Particles move faster in hotter substances than in colder ones.

f Would a stink bomb spread quicker on a cold day or a hot day? Explain why.

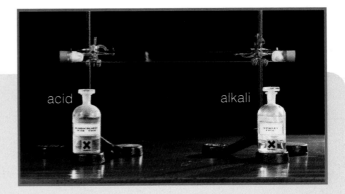

acid   alkali

Questions

1. Use the particle model to explain why diffusion is quicker in a gas than a liquid.

2. **a** Small, light particles diffuse faster than large, heavy particles. Explain why this happens.
   b In the experiment in the photo opposite, a white ring will form where the particles of acid and alkali meet and react. The white ring forms nearer to the acid than the alkali. Which has lighter particles, the acid or the alkali? Explain your answer.

3. Do you think diffusion can happen in a solid? Explain your answer.

4. Many perfumes are made using special solvents that evaporate very easily. Explain why this might be a useful property.

5. Helen noticed that her green bubble bath spread quicker in a hot bath than it did in a cold bath. Explain to her why this happens.

For your notes

Substances spread out in a gas or a liquid as their particles move and mix. This is called **diffusion**.

Diffusion happens faster in hotter substances than in colder ones. This is because the particles are moving faster.

Size matters

Mercury rising

The photo shows a thermometer. Some thermometers contain a metal called mercury. Mercury is different from most metals because it is a liquid at room temperature.

When it is hot, the mercury appears to move up the thermometer.

When it is cold, the mercury appears to move down the thermometer.

The particle theory can be used to explain why this happens.

Expanding

As the mercury is heated up, its particles are given thermal energy. This energy is changed into kinetic energy. This means that the particles move around more and take up more space.

Because each particle takes up more space, the column of mercury gets longer. We say it has **expanded**. The column gets longer because it only has space to expand upwards. The tube prevents it from expanding in other directions.

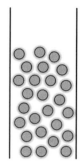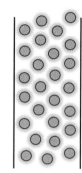

At lower temperatures, the particles only vibrate a little.

At higher temperatures, the particles are the same size but they vibrate more and take up more space. The mercury expands.

Contracting

If you cool the mercury down, the opposite happens. The particles lose kinetic energy. They vibrate less and take up less space.

Because each particle takes up less space, the mercury column gets shorter. We say that it has **contracted**.

Expanding bridges

Engineers need to understand expansion and contraction in solids when they build things. Changes in temperature can affect the way building materials behave.

In some railway lines there is a gap between the pieces of track to give the metal room to expand on hot days. If the gaps were not there, the track would buckle and bend. Motorways also have gaps between sections of concrete for the same reason. The gaps are filled with tar which can be squashed.

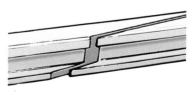

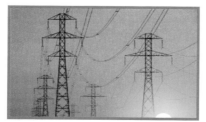

Power cables are never tight between pylons. There is always some slack in the cable. This means that on very cold days, when the cable contracts, it does not pull the pylons together.

The ends of many bridges are not fixed to the rest of the road. There are gaps at the ends to allow the bridge to expand. Sometimes the ends are placed on rollers to help them move as they expand.

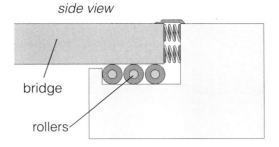
side view

bridge

rollers

a Why are there gaps between some types of railway track?

b What would happen if the bridge was fixed at both ends?

Two different materials

Not all materials expand by the same amount. Some expand more than others.

The picture shows a **bimetallic strip**. This is made from a strip of iron joined to a strip of brass.

As the two metals are heated, they expand. The brass expands more than the iron. Because the metals are joined together, the bimetallic strip bends. The strip straightens out again when it is cooled.

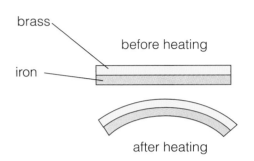
brass

before heating

iron

after heating

c Suggest two devices in which a bimetallic strip might be used.

Questions

1. Steve was cooking oven chips. His baking tray went into the hot oven easily. When he tried to get the tray out later it was jammed inside the oven. Explain in detail why this happened.

2. Explain how you could use heat to release a tight jam jar lid.

3. The diagram shows a bimetallic strip being used in an electrical circuit with a heater.
   a Explain what will happen as the strip gets hotter.
   b What do you think this circuit could be used for?

4. Rivets are used to hold pieces of metal together. The rivets are heated up, then put through holes in the metal. The end is then flattened off.
   a What will happen to the rivet as it cools down?
   b What will happen to the metal sheets?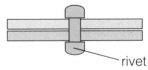
   rivet

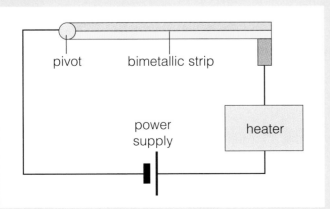
pivot   bimetallic strip

power supply

heater

For your notes

When you heat a substance, the particles vibrate more and take up more space. The substance **expands**.

When you cool a substance, the particles vibrate less and take up less space. The substance **contracts**.

Different materials expand and contract by different amounts.

Under pressure

Pump it up

Inside this balloon are millions of air particles. The gas particles are moving around in all directions. Quite often these particles bump into the sides of the balloon. Every time they hit the side of the balloon they give the rubber a tiny push, and transfer some energy to it. Each push is quite small, but lots of particles all pushing at the same time adds up to quite a lot of force. The force against the side of the balloon exerts **gas pressure**. The balloon is kept in shape by the pressure of the gas inside it.

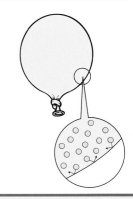

Air pressure

Air is a gas. The gas particles are all around us and we are always being hit by them. They cause **air pressure** (or atmospheric pressure). We don't usually feel the air pressure because the pressure within our bodies balances the pressure outside.

Wind is caused by air rushing from an area of high pressure to an area of low pressure. We see this when air rushes out of a hole in a balloon.

(a) Explain why air rushes out of hole in a balloon by comparing the pressure inside the balloon and the air pressure outside.

Did you know?

The pneumatic (gas-filled) bicycle tyre was invented by John Dunlop in **1888**. Before this, tyres were made of solid rubber and riding a bike was quite an uncomfortable experience!

Heat it up

If you heat a gas inside a syringe, the particles have more kinetic energy and so they move around faster and try to move further apart. This means that they hit the sides of the syringe more often and harder than before. The pressure of the gas inside the syringe increases if you hold the plunger still.

The air pressure outside remains the same. If you let the plunger go, the force on the inside of the plunger is now greater than the force on the outside. The plunger moves out so that the gas pressure inside equals the air pressure outside. The forces on the plunger are now balanced. The gas has expanded.

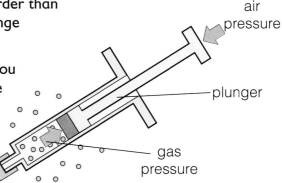

(b) What do you think would happen to the plunger if the gas got colder? Explain your answer.

When you heat a gas in a syringe, it becomes less dense. This is because there are still the same number of particles, but they have moved further apart, so they take up a bigger volume.

Going up

The air inside this hot air balloon is heated using gas burners. In the heated air, the gas particles move apart and the air expands. The air inside the balloon is less dense than the air outside it. This makes the balloon rise in the air.

To keep the balloon flying, the pilot turns the burners on from time to time to keep the air hot. To land the balloon, the pilot opens a gap in the top of the balloon so the hot air rushes out.

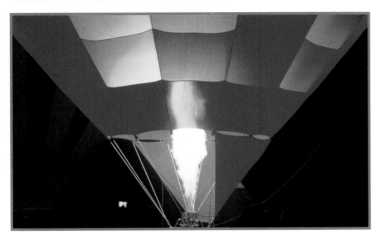

c Draw a diagram to show how the air particles are arranged inside and outside the balloon when it is flying.

Too much pressure

If you heat a gas inside a container that cannot get bigger, then the gas pressure will increase. If the gas gets too hot, and the pressure gets too high, then the container may explode.

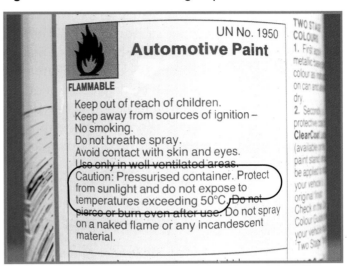

Questions

1. The label on a deodorant can says: 'Do not expose to temperatures above 50 °C.' Explain why, using the words 'particles' and 'pressure' in your explanation.

2. Use the particle theory to explain the benefits of John Dunlop's pneumatic tyres.

3. Dot noticed that the tyres on her bike were harder on a hot day than they were on a cold day. Why do you think this happens?

4. If you squash a gas, its pressure will go up. Use your knowledge of particles to explain this. You may need to use diagrams to help you.

5. Think about the syringe experiment. What is the relationship between the temperature of a gas and its volume if you let the plunger move?

For your notes

Gas pressure is caused by the gas particles hitting the sides of the container.

When you heat a gas, the particles hit the sides of the container more and the pressure goes up. When you cool the gas, the pressure goes down.

If you heat a gas in a container that can get bigger, the gas expands. It becomes less dense.

Air pressure is caused by air particles all around us and we are always being hit by them.

As the temperature of a gas in a syringe goes up, the volume increases. As the temperature goes down, the volume decreases.

Solubility

Why is it soluble?

The photo shows copper sulfate dissolving in water. The diagram below shows that the copper sulfate solution contains particles from the copper sulfate (blue), each surrounded by water molecules (white).

In copper sulfate, there are forces of attraction between the copper sulfate particles. The water molecules have enough energy to be able to break these particles apart. Water molecules surround the copper sulfate particles. The dissolved particles are then held by tiny forces of attraction with the water molecules, and these forces of attraction release energy. The energy given out when these forces of attraction are made 'pays back' almost all the energy that was needed to break the copper sulfate particles apart.

Learn about

► Dissolving

► Solubility

Saturation and solubility

You can add more and more copper sulfate crystals until no more will dissolve. The solution is then saturated. There does not seem to be enough energy to break the forces of attraction between any more copper sulfate particles at that particular temperature.

Scientists measure what mass of a substance will dissolve in 100 cm³ of solvent at a certain temperature. This is called the **solubility** of the substance. Each substance has a different solubility. In most cases, the solubility of a solid increases when the temperature rises.

Where does it go?

Mass of salt.   *Mass of water.*   *Mass of salt solution.*

Look at the photos. Matter is still there when you make a solution. You have the same mass of solute and solvent as you started with. We say that the mass has been **conserved**. You have not lost any particles, so you do not lose any mass.

Different temperatures

The solubility of a substance depends on the temperature of the solvent. The graph shows how much of substances **X** and **Y** will dissolve in 100 cm³ of water at different temperatures. The hotter the solvent, the more energy there is available to overcome the forces of attraction in the solid lattice.

Look at the graph on the opposite page.

a   i   How much of substance **X** dissolves at 70°C?
      ii   How much of substance **Y** dissolves at 10°C?
     iii   Which substance is the more soluble at 60°C?

Temperature also affects how quickly a substance will dissolve. At higher temperatures, the solvent molecules have more energy and move more quickly. The solvent molecules hit the lumps of solid more often and harder, knocking off the outer particles more easily.

Cooling off

When a saturated solution cools, the dissolving process is reversed. Crystals begin to grow and the solute comes out of solution.

Look at the graph on the opposite page.

b   i   How much of substance **X** dissolves at 80°C?
      ii   How much of substance **X** dissolves at 55°C?
     iii   How much of substance **X** would crystallise out if you cooled a saturated solution from 80°C to 55°C?

Different solvents

Different solutes dissolve in different solvents. For example, salt dissolves in water but not in petrol. For a substance to dissolve, there must be a force of attraction between the solute particles and the solvent molecules.

There are hardly any forces of attraction between salt particles and petrol molecules. This means that not enough energy is given out to 'pay back' the energy needed to break apart the particles in the salt crystals. Salt is insoluble in petrol.

Differences in solubility allow scientists to separate mixtures by the process of chromatography. The chromatograms below show ink from two different pens. The experiment was carried out with two different solvents, water and ethanol.

c   Which pen would you use to label clothes? Explain your answer.

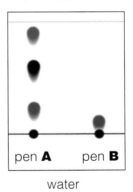 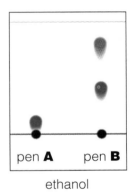

water   ethanol

Questions

1. What is meant by 'solubility'?

2. Use the solubility table to answer these questions.

Substance	Solubility in g per 100 cm³ of water at 25°C
Magnesium sulfate	43
Sodium chloride	36
Copper sulfate	22
Magnesium chloride	53

   a   How much magnesium chloride will dissolve in 500 cm³ of water?
   b   Can you make a saturated solution by adding 10 g of copper sulfate to 50 cm³ of water? Explain your answer.

3. In pen **A** above, which coloured dye is most soluble in water? Explain your answer.

For your notes

Solubility is the amount of a substance that will dissolve.

The solubility of a substance changes with temperature.

Mass is always **conserved** when solutions are formed.

Some substances are insoluble in certain solvents.

Scientific models

Models

The word 'model' can mean lots of different things to us. You might think of a fashion model on a catwalk, or a model aeroplane or you might model clay. When scientists talk about a model, they mean a way of representing how something works or looks that they cannot see or touch.

Christmas presents

On Christmas Eve, Jackie's six-year-old brother Matt had gone to bed. Jackie was looking at the presents for him under the Christmas tree to see if she could tell what they were. She couldn't open them, but she wanted to try and find out what was in them.

a What could she do with the presents, apart from open them, that would help her collect more information about what they are like?

Eventually, Jackie decided that one of the presents could be a book or a video.

b Make a table to describe some of the ways a book and a video are similar, and some of the ways they are different.

After shaking it, feeling it and testing its weight, Jackie decided it was a video. She had collected her evidence and used her model of a video to explain what she could hear and feel inside the present.

Scientific models

Scientists use models in a similar way to help them think about how things work or behave. First they think about the evidence they have, and then they use a model that might explain it. You have met the particle model in this unit. Now try using it to explain the five following events.

(1) Feeling the cold

This balloon was inflated with air and then dunked into liquid nitrogen (**A**). Liquid nitrogen is very cold indeed. When the balloon was taken out of the liquid nitrogen (**B**) it was a lot smaller.

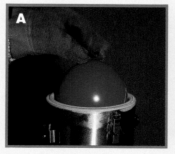
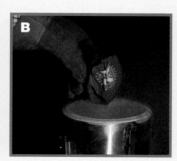

c Use the particle model to explain what is happening in the photos.

d Use the particle model to predict what will happen to the balloon as it warms up again.

(2) Glass-blowing

The person in the photo is making a bottle by a process called glass-blowing. A ball of glass is heated until it is red-hot. When it is hot, the glass can be stretched or shaped. This makes it easy to shape the glass into a bottle. The glass is then left to cool.

e What does this tell you about the particles in the glass when it is hot?

f Suggest what is different about the arrangement of the glass particles in the cold glass bottle and in the hot ball of glass.

(3) Sublimation

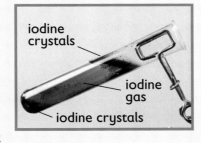

iodine crystals

iodine gas

iodine crystals

The photo shows what happens when iodine crystals are heated gently over a Bunsen burner flame. Iodine does not form a liquid. It changes straight from a solid to a gas. Scientists call this **sublimation**. Crystals of iodine are forming again at the top the glass tube, where it is colder.

g Look carefully at the photo. Use the particle model to explain what is happening to the iodine:
  i when it is heated
  ii when it cools again.

(4) Gassy problem

The gas that comes out of the gas tap is called methane. On Earth, methane is usually a gas, but there are some places where methane looks very different. The planet Uranus has liquid methane on its surface.

h What does this information tell you about the temperature on Uranus?

i Use your knowledge of the particle model to explain what would happen to the methane on Uranus if it got warmer.

(5) Breaking point

The photos show a metal rod being tested to see how strong it is. The machine exerts a very strong pulling force on the metal. The pulling force is gradually increased until the metal rod finally snaps.

j For each of the three photos, use your knowledge of the particle model to explain what is happening to the particles in the metal rod.

Questions

1. The polar ice-caps on the planet Mars are made from solid carbon dioxide. Carbon dioxide behaves in the same way as iodine. Use your knowledge of the particle model to explain why Mars would not flood if the planet warmed up.

2. Explain why scientists often need to use models to describe what is happening.

3. Glass panes in windows which are hundreds of years old get thicker at the bottom of the pane and thinner at the top. What does this tell you about glass?

4. Why may it be dangerous to add very hot water to very cold glass?

Getting food

All animals and plants need food. Food gives them the energy they need to carry out their life processes. Plants make their own food by photosynthesis. Animals have to find their food. It is easy for people in the developed world to get food. We just go to the nearest supermarket.

As you go around most supermarkets you will see many different types of fruits and vegetables from all around the world. You can see bananas from the Caribbean, green beans from Africa, cheese from England and Holland and meat from Wales and New Zealand.

a Why do we import food from different countries?

b Why is it less efficient to import food than to grow our own?

Sometimes labels on the food give you information about what you are buying. You may have noticed that some labels say 'organic' or 'organically grown', like the ones opposite.

A few years ago there were very few organic fruits and vegetables in supermarkets. Now you will see many different organically grown food products.

Organic food

Organic is a word used to describe food that has been grown without using manufactured chemicals. Farms that are not organic may use chemicals such as:

- **fertilisers** to keep the soil fertile
- **pesticides** to kill insects or other pests that grow on the crops and damage them
- **hormones** to make animals grow faster, or fruits ripen earlier.

Organic farms do not use these chemicals.

Why people want organic food

Some people want organically grown food because it is better for the environment. It does not damage wildlife because chemical pesticides are not used. Getting rid of pests from crops can leave other animals such as birds without food.

Some people want organic food because it is healthier. Organic food does not contain any manufactured chemicals. There may be small amounts of these chemicals left behind in non-organic food. Organic farm workers do not have to use powerful chemicals that may cause health problems such as asthma.

Organic farming methods keep the soil more fertile. Natural fertilisers such as manure are used. Fields are left to rest, or different crops are grown that take out different substances from the soil. This allows the soil to recover and become fertile again.

Organically produced animals such as pigs are kept in surroundings more like their natural habitat. They are given more space to live in and sometimes given toys to play with to keep them happy.

Disadvantages of organic food

Without manufactured pesticides and hormones, the amount of crop produced on an organic farm may be reduced, as some of the crop may be spoiled by pests and diseases. This can increase the price of organic food.

The world's human population is six billion and rising. Many people think that the only way to feed everyone in the world is to use more efficient non-organic farming methods.

Non-organic farmers use wax to coat their fruits, and food dyes to make their food look nice. Organic products may take longer to grow and may be attacked by insects. This means that organic food often does not look as good as non-organic food.

c Which do you think is easier, putting a chemical fertiliser on a field or farming it organically to keep it fertile?

Getting more organic

In 2000, only about 0.5% of land in the UK was farmed organically, compared with about 4% in Germany, 5% in Denmark and 8% in Austria. About 70% of organic food bought in the UK was imported from European countries and the USA. More and more organic food is being grown in the UK to meet the rising demand.

Questions

1. Use the following words to write a paragraph about organic food.

   > **chemicals animals cost
   > future nature farming**

2. Make a table to list the disadvantages and advantages of organic farming.

3. Use the figures on this page to make a bar chart comparing the amount of land used for organic farming in different European countries.

4. Discuss what you think is going to happen to organic farming in the future.

5. Design a leaflet explaining why people might consider buying organic food.

What's in food?

What are nutrients?

Food contains many different substances. The useful substances that food contains are called **nutrients**. Look at the food label shown below.

NUTRITION		
TYPICAL COMPOSITION	A 30g serving with 125ml semi-skimmed milk provides	100g (3¹/₂oz) provide
Energy	718kJ/170kcal*	1560kJ/367kcal
Protein	6.3 g	7.3 g
Carbohydrate of which sugars	31.1 g 8.9 g	82.7 g 8.9 g
Fat of which saturates	2.2 g* 1.5 g	0.8 g 0.3 g
Fibre**	1.1 g	3.6 g
Sodium	0.4 g	1.1 g
VITAMINS/MINERALS		
Vitamin D	1.6μg (32% RDA)	5.0μg (100% RDA)
Thiamin	0.5mg (34% RDA)	1.4mg (100% RDA)
Riboflavin	0.7mg (44% RDA)	1.6mg (100% RDA)
Niacin	6.5mg (36% RDA)	18.0mg (100% RDA)
Vitamin B₆	0.7mg (34% RDA)	2.0mg (100% RDA)
Folic acid	127.5μg (63% RDA)	400.0μg (200% RDA)
Vitamin B₁₂	0.8μg (80% RDA)	1.0μg (100% RDA)
Pantothenic acid	2.2mg (37% RDA)	6.0mg (100% RDA)
Iron	4.3mg (30% RDA)	14.0mg (100% RDA)
RDA = Recommended Daily Allowance		
This pack contains approx 16 servings		
INFORMATION		

*Calories/Fat per serving with whole milk: 195 cals/5g

a What are the main types of nutrient listed in this food?

The main nutrients – carbohydrates, fats and protein

Carbohydrates give you energy. They are found in bread, potatoes, cakes and sweets. Sugar and starch are both carbohydrates.

Fats also give you energy. Fat insulates your body. Fats are found in butter, margarine, full fat milk and meat.

Proteins help your body to grow and repair itself. They are found in meat, fish, eggs, peas, beans and milk.

Small amounts – vitamins and minerals

Vitamins are needed in very small amounts to keep the body healthy. Different vitamins have different jobs. If a vitamin is missing from someone's diet, it can cause a disease. We say that the person is **deficient** in that vitamin.

Vitamin A is found in carrots and helps to keep your skin and eyes healthy.

Vitamin C is found in fruit and green vegetables. Sailors on long voyages used to become deficient in vitamin C because they did not eat any fresh food. They got the disease **scurvy**. Their gums bled and their teeth fell out. If they cut themselves, the skin did not heal.

b Sailors on long voyages today do not get scurvy. What do you think has changed?

Vitamin D is found in milk and butter. It is also made by your body in sunlight. Vitamin D gives you strong bones and teeth. If this vitamin is deficient it can cause a disease called **rickets** where the bones are soft.

Another vitamin is called **vitamin B12**. This is often missing from the diet of vegetarians as it is not found in plants. Without vitamin B12 people can get a disease called **anaemia**. They feel tired as they have fewer red blood cells to carry oxygen. Oxygen is needed to release the energy in your food so you can use it.

Your body also needs **minerals** in small amounts. Different minerals have different functions.

Calcium is a mineral found in milk and cheese. You need calcium for healthy teeth and bones. **Iron** is found in liver and eggs and is used to make blood. If iron is missing

from the diet it can cause anaemia. Another mineral called **iodine** is found in foods such as fish. The thyroid gland in the neck uses iodine to produce a hormone that makes you grow. People who do not have enough iodine can get a disease called **goitre**. The thyroid gland becomes very large, as you can see in the photo.

Fibre and water

Fibre is also needed in your diet. Fibre is sometimes called **roughage** and it is found in cereals, fruit and vegetables. It helps food to keep moving through the gut. Fibre prevents you from becoming constipated and may reduce the risk of some types of cancer.

c Fibre comes from plants. Think about the differences between animal cells and plant cells. What do you think gives plants this fibre?

You take in **water** when you eat and drink. You would die in a few days without water. All the chemical reactions in your body take place in water.

Did you know?

Your body loses about $2\frac{1}{2}$ litres of water a day, most of it as urine.

Did you know?

At some periods in history females with goitres were thought to look attractive.

Questions

1. Explain the meaning of the following words. Give examples of each.
   a deficient   **b** fibre   **c** mineral

2. Write a list of all the foods you eat in a whole day. Say how you could improve your diet in the future.

3. Which foods mentioned on these pages would contain the following nutrients?
   a protein, fat and calcium
   b protein and fibre
   c protein and iron

4. Design a quiz sheet for other pupils in your class about all the different nutrients in the human diet. Include questions and answers on your sheet.

For your notes

Food contains useful substances called **nutrients**.

The main types of nutrient in food are **carbohydrates**, **fats**, **proteins**, **vitamins** and **minerals**.

Fibre and **water** are also needed for a healthy diet.

Getting the balance right

Your body needs nutrients for energy and to keep it working properly so you stay fit and healthy. A diet that has the right amounts of all the nutrients is called a **balanced diet**. A balanced diet gives you the right amounts of carbohydrates, fats, proteins, vitamins, minerals, fibre and water.

How much should we eat?

Government scientists advise us how much of each nutrient we should eat a day. They set **recommended daily intakes (RDI)** or **recommended daily allowances (RDA)** for some of the nutrients and energy that make up a balanced diet. The table below shows some RDAs for different people.

(a) Describe any differences between:
  i males and females
  ii children and adults.

(b) i What differences can you see in the RDA for iron?
  ii Can you explain this?

Person (age in years)	Energy in kJ	Protein in g	Vitamin A in µg	Vitamin C in mg	Iron in mg
Male 10–12	10 900	30	575	20	5–10
Female 10–12	9800	29	575	20	5–10
Adult male	12 600	37	750	30	5–9
Adult female	9200	29	750	30	14–28

Balancing the energy

The amount of energy in food you need a day depends on how much energy your body uses. This depends on whether you are growing, how active you are and the size of your body. Men need more energy than women. A teenage boy uses about 12 500 kJ of energy every day, while a girl of the same age uses about 10 000 kJ. A person doing a very active job such as a builder uses a lot more energy than an office worker of the same age and sex.

It is important to take in the right amount of energy in your food. Some people take in more energy than they use up. They risk becoming fat. People who are very overweight for their height are called **obese**.

Some people do not eat enough food to give them energy for their body's needs and they lose weight. Obese people may eat less in order to lose weight.

You should always speak to your doctor before going on a diet. Sometimes people can suffer from eating disorders such as **anorexia nervosa**. They do not eat enough and they become very underweight. This disease can kill.

Different diets

We have seen that different people need different amounts of energy every day. Some people also need different nutrients to stay healthy.

Pregnant women need to be careful what they eat and drink as it may affect the developing fetus.

Pregnant women are advised to supplement their diets with folic acid. This helps prevent certain kinds of disability in the baby. Women also need extra nutrients in the last three months of pregnancy. They may take extra calcium for the growing bones of the fetus, protein for its muscles and cells and iron for its blood.

c What do you think 'supplement' means?

Sports people use a lot of energy and they need to take in energy very quickly. They often use drinks that contain a lot of sugars such as glucose that can be used for energy very quickly.

Vegetarians do not eat any meat. To give them a balanced diet they eat nuts, seeds and cereals to give them protein. Some vegetarians are known as **vegans**. These people have a diet that contains no animal products such as cheese or butter. Balanced vegetarian diets can be very healthy as they contain less fat and more fibre than a diet including meat.

People from different cultures eat different foods. This may be due to religion, tradition or simply what is available in the country. In many Asian countries such as China the main food is rice. In some countries in Africa the main food is maize. In developed countries such as the UK the diet often contains too much fat and is also high in salt. A person who eats a high-fat diet is more likely to have a heart attack. A diet high in salt can increase the risk of having strokes. This kind of diet is often termed the 'Western diet'.

Questions

1. Jake is a vegetarian. His friend Zoe enjoys eating burgers and chips. Jake thinks that his diet is probably more healthy than Zoe's. Explain why he may be correct.

2. There are no RDIs or RDAs for carbohydrate or fats in Western countries.
   a Why do you think this is the case?
   b Why are carbohydrates and fats important for the diet?

3. Decide whether you think each of these statements is **true** or **false**. Explain your decisions.
   a An office worker uses less energy than a builder.
   b Vegetarians are at risk of eating too little roughage.
   c Athletes need lots of glucose when they compete.
   d The 'Western diet' is very healthy.

Did you know?

Thirty per cent of the population of the USA are officially considered to be obese.

4. Design a newsletter to inform pregnant women what they need to eat to ensure their babies are healthy when they are born.

For your notes

A diet that has the right amount of each nutrient is called a **balanced diet**.

It is important to balance the energy in your food with the energy your body uses.

The digestive system

The start

Food contains nutrients, but to get the nutrients into our bodies the food must be broken down into smaller molecules that can get into the blood. This process is called **digestion**.

Digestion starts in the mouth where the food is broken up into smaller pieces by the teeth. The human mouth contains front teeth called **incisors** and back teeth called **molars**. Incisors are used for cutting food and molars for chewing. There are also **canine** teeth for piercing and tearing meat. Chopping up food in this way is a physical process.

(a) Sheep do not have canine teeth. Why do you think this is?

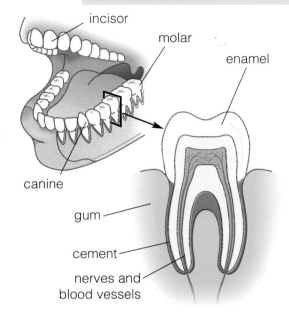

Down the tube

The **digestive system** includes all the organs that take part in digestion, shown in the diagram opposite.

After the food leaves the mouth it passes through a tube called the **gut** which is 9 metres long. The first part of the tube is called the **gullet** or **oesophagus**. This links the mouth and stomach. The oesophagus has muscular walls that push the food down using movements called **peristalsis**. You can imagine peristalsis as being like a tennis ball being pushed down an empty pair of tights.

Involuntary muscle in the oesophagus makes peristalsis happen. There are two layers of this muscle, one running around the oesophagus wall and the other running along the length of it. They contract and relax to push the food through.

In the **stomach** the food is churned up for a few hours by its muscular walls. Digestive juices are added. These contain **enzymes** and acid. Enzymes are proteins. They are made by the body to help break down the food into smaller molecules.

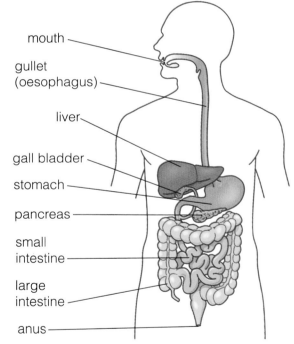

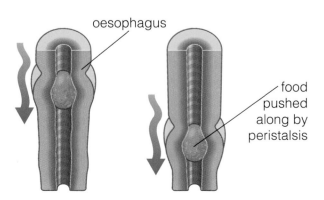

Each different enzyme acts on a particular food substance. The acidic conditions in the stomach kill germs and make the enzymes work at their best.

After a few hours the food has become a runny liquid. This leaves the stomach and enters the **small intestine**. This is a long tube where three different liquids are added:

● pancreatic juice made by the pancreas
● bile from the gall bladder in the liver
● intestinal juice.

Pancreatic and intestinal juices contain enzymes which digest several different types of nutrients. These enzymes work best in alkaline conditions. Bile is alkaline so it neutralises the acid from the stomach. It also helps to break down fats.

 Explain why:
   i acid is needed in the stomach
   ii the acid then needs to be neutralised.

An absorbing process

The digested food is now made up of small molecules. These pass through the lining of the small intestine into the blood. This process is called **absorption**. The digested food molecules are taken away in the blood to where they are needed.

The small intestine has millions of tiny finger-like structures called **villi** (singular **villus**) on its surface, as shown in the photo. The villi make the surface area of the small intestine much larger. The large surface makes sure that the digested food is absorbed quickly.

c Explain the function of the villi.

What's left?

Some undigested food, mainly fibre, is left in the small intestine. We do not have any enzymes to digest fibre. It is not absorbed into the blood because its molecules are too big to pass through the lining of the small intestine. It passes into the **large intestine**. Here the waste food can be stored, and water is absorbed from it into the blood to be used by the body. Later the waste is pushed out of the body through the **anus**. This process is called **egestion**.

The waste that is egested is called **faeces**. Faeces contain not only undigested food but also lots of dead cells and microorganisms from the gut.

Questions

1. Explain the meaning of the following words:
   a egestion **b** fibre **c** peristalsis.

2. Explain why bile is important in digestion.

3. The small intestine is one of the longest parts of the gut. It is folded up inside the body. Why do you think it is so long and folded?

4. If you were a doctor, how would you test to see whether the stomach was acidic and the small intestine was alkaline?

5. Draw a flow chart to show the parts of the digestive system that food passes through in order. Start at the mouth and finish at the anus.

6. Write a poem about the journey of the food through the gut.

For your notes

Digestion takes place in the **digestive system**.

This consists of the **mouth, oesophagus, stomach, small intestine, large intestine** and **anus**.

Small molecules of digested food are **absorbed** into the blood.

69

Enzymes

5.5

Nutrition

Total breakdown

In the mouth, the teeth help break up the food into smaller pieces. This mechanical breakdown of the food is a physical process.

When we **digest** food, the small pieces of food are broken down even further into substances with very small molecules. Only small molecules can be absorbed through the lining of the small intestine into the blood. Large molecules cannot pass through the lining. Breaking down food into smaller molecules is a chemical process.

Learn about

► Enzymes

► Absorption

a Outline the difference between a chemical process and a physical process.

b Give another example of a physical process that you know about.

Enzymes – chemical breakers

In digestion, chemicals called **enzymes** help to break the larger molecules into smaller molecules. Enzymes make the digestion of food happen more quickly. Enzymes for digesting food are found in the mouth, stomach and small intestine.

c Why do you think it is important for food to be digested quickly?

Each enzyme helps break down a different type of nutrient. Some break down carbohydrates, some break down proteins and others break down fats.

There are large carbohydrate molecules such as starch in foods like bread, rice and pasta. These are broken down into small **glucose** molecules.

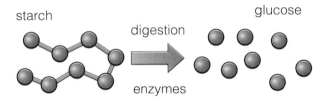

There are large protein molecules in foods such as eggs, meat and fish. These are broken down into small molecules called **amino acids**.

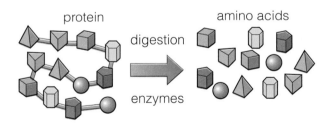

There are fats in foods such as butter and oils. These are broken down into smaller molecules called **fatty acids** and **glycerol**.

Naming enzymes

Enzymes in digestion are normally named after the substances they break down. The name of an enzyme ends in the letters '-ase'. So enzymes that break down:

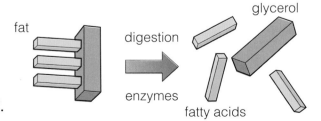

- carbohydrates are called carbohydr**ase**s
- proteins are called prote**ase**s
- fats (lipids) are called lip**ase**s
- starch (amylose) are called amyl**ase**s.

More about absorption

Look at the diagram opposite. Small molecules such as glucose can pass through the wall of the gut. They pass into the blood to be carried away to the parts of the body where they are needed. Large starch molecules need to be broken down to smaller glucose molecules before they can be absorbed.

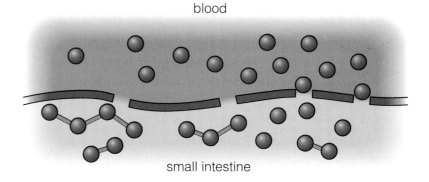

blood

small intestine

Did you know?

Some washing powders are described as 'biological', and others are 'non-biological'. **Biological washing powders** contain enzymes such as protease that help to clean dirty clothes.

Some substances in food such as minerals and vitamins are small enough to go straight through the gut wall. Other substances such as fibre cannot be broken down as there are no enzymes to do it.

d Look again at the diagram above showing small molecules getting into the blood. Try to think of two ideas you could use as models to explain absorption. The picture opposite will give you a clue for one model.

Questions

1. Explain why digestion is both a chemical and a physical process.

2. Write a paragraph to explain the action of enzymes in digestion. Include all the words below in your paragraph.

   > protease   amylase   absorption   villi   glucose

3. What do you think is the main enzyme needed to break down each of the following foods?
   a fish **b** bread **c** butter **d** rice, which is rich in starch

4. Milly says scurvy is caused by people not having an enzyme to digest vitamin C. Do you agree with her? Explain your answer.

5. Design a poster to show what happens when foods are broken down by enzymes.

For your notes

Digestion uses physical and chemical processes to break down food into smaller molecules.

Enzymes speed up the breakdown of food.

Different enzymes work on different nutrients.

Food for energy

Food and energy

Food gives you energy. Carbohydrates, fats and proteins provide your body with the energy you need to stay healthy. The energy is used for many things such as working your muscles and organs, transporting chemicals, growing and repairing cells and keeping your body temperature constant. Your food is the fuel that keeps you going.

Fuels and respiration

When a fuel such as petrol or natural gas is burned, chemical energy is transferred to light energy and thermal energy. The fuel reacts with oxygen to produce carbon dioxide and water, and energy is released. Your body uses a similar reaction to get the energy from food. It is called **respiration**.

The fuel used in respiration is glucose. The glucose comes from the digestion of food. What other substances are involved in respiration, and where do they come from? The table shows the gases that are in the air when you breathe in and out.

a Look at the table.
  i Suggest which gas is used in respiration.
  ii Suggest which gases are made by respiration.
  iii How did you come to your conclusions?

Gas	% in air breathed in	% in air breathed out
Nitrogen	78	78
Oxygen	21	16
Carbon dioxide	0.04	4
Water vapour	Variable	Variable but a lot more

The oxygen for respiration comes from the air you breathe in. Carbon dioxide, water and energy are produced by respiration. The waste carbon dioxide and water are added to the air you breathe out.

Respiration can be shown in a word equation:

glucose + oxygen → carbon dioxide + water

energy given out

b What are the reactants and products in respiration?

Where does respiration happen?

Respiration takes place in all living cells. It happens in small structures called **mitochondria** inside the cells. Some cells, such as muscle cells, need lots of energy. They have lots of mitochondria to carry out respiration and supply the energy.

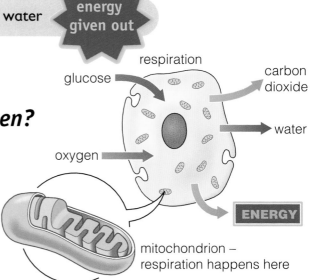

respiration

glucose

carbon dioxide

water

oxygen

ENERGY

mitochondrion – respiration happens here

Transport for respiration

In larger organisms the oxygen and glucose needed for respiration are transported to the cells by the blood. Look at the photo of red blood cells. Oxygen travels attached to a special chemical called **haemoglobin** in red blood cells, and glucose is dissolved in the watery part of the blood. Oxygen and glucose can pass from the blood to nearby cells where they are needed.

The waste products from respiration are carbon dioxide and water. The water may be used in the cell, or it may pass into the blood to be taken away. Carbon dioxide is taken away dissolved in the blood.

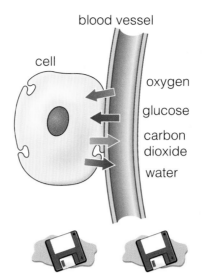

blood vessel

cell

oxygen
glucose
carbon dioxide
water

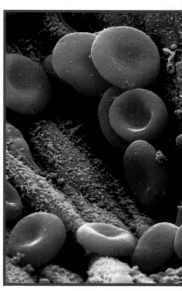

Respiration for exercise

Look at the word equation for respiration. Oxygen is needed for this type of respiration. It is called **aerobic** respiration. There is also another type of respiration that does not use oxygen. This is called **anaerobic** respiration. In animals, anaerobic respiration produces **lactic acid**.

During exercise, the body needs more energy and the rate of respiration increases. Sometimes during vigorous exercise such as sprinting, not enough oxygen can be supplied to your muscles so they cannot carry out aerobic respiration. Instead they carry out anaerobic respiration. Glucose is broken down to lactic acid and energy is released, but not as much as in aerobic respiration.

In plants and yeast, anaerobic respiration produces **ethanol** (alcohol). The yeast shown in the photo on the right carries out anaerobic respiration called **fermentation** to get energy.

Questions

1. Why is respiration so important to all organisms?

2. How is respiration the same as burning wood?

3. Explain why the levels of nitrogen are the same in air breathed in and in air breathed out.

4. All the windows in the science block are jammed shut. One small room in the block is full of people for several hours of science lessons. A similar room next door has just one person in it. What do you think would be different about the air in the two rooms?

For your notes

Respiration is the process by which living things get energy from food.

Aerobic respiration can be summarised by the equation:

glucose + oxygen → carbon dioxide + water

energy given out

Anaerobic respiration occurs without oxygen.

Chewing it over

Digestion of starch

Wendy took a bite of her baguette. She thought, 'The bigger the bite, the more starch there is to be digested, and the longer it takes …'.

Wendy wanted to find out whether adding a bigger amount of an enzyme to starch speeds up digestion. Starch is broken down (digested) into glucose by an enzyme called salivary amylase, which is produced in your mouth.

She used the same amount of starch each time, but added different amounts of the enzyme. She used iodine indicator to show when the starch had disappeared. She timed how long it took for the starch to disappear each time. When the starch had disappeared, she knew it had all been digested.

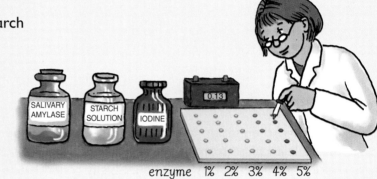

enzyme 1% 2% 3% 4% 5%

Her results are shown in the table. The concentration tells you the amount of amylase enzyme she added. For example, 1 cm³ of 2% enzyme contains twice as much enzyme as 1 cm³ of 1% enzyme.

Wendy wanted to see if there was a pattern in her results, so she drew a line graph. Line graphs help you see the relationship between variables in an experiment.

Amount (concentration) of salivary amylase in %	Time taken to digest all the starch in seconds
1	240
2	210
3	160
4	115
5	80

Wendy put the input variable (the amount of enzyme used) along the bottom, on the x-axis. She put the outcome variable (the time taken to digest the starch) up the side, on the y-axis. She plotted her results on the graph.

a Draw axes like Wendy did and plot her results.

b Can you draw a straight line through all the crosses?

Lines of best fit

In many experiments, you cannot draw a line that passes through all the points. You have to draw a line that fits most of them. This is called the **line of best fit**.

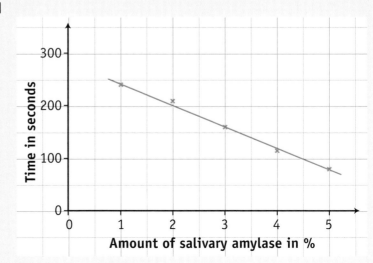

c Why do you think that lines on graphs do not always go through all the points?

Wendy's graph is shown on the previous page, with her line of best fit.

d What pattern do you see in the results?

e Describe the relationship between the input variable and the outcome variable.

Interpreting graphs

Drawing a line of best fit helps you see the **trend** or general pattern of the results. Then you can see the relationship between the input variable and the outcome variable.

Wendy used her graph to predict how long it would probably take for other concentrations of amylase to digest starch. She drew a line up to the graph from 1.5% on the x-axis, and read off the time on the y-axis.

f Do this on your copy of Wendy's graph. What is the time on the y-axis?

g Why do you think she would want to do this?

She can also extend the line and predict how fast starch will be digested by a 6.5% concentration of amylase.

h Do this on your copy of Wendy's graph. How long will it take for the starch to be digested by a 6.5% concentration of amylase?

Other relationships

Charlotte decided to look at the way pH affects how an enzyme works. She used the same concentration of amylase for all her tests, but she changed the pH of the starch solution by adding acid or alkali. She recorded the time it took for the starch to be digested. Her results are shown in the table opposite.

i Use the data in the table to plot a graph. Try to draw a curve of best fit to join the points.

j Describe the relationship shown by your graph in terms of how the time taken to digest the starch changes with pH.

The relationship shown by the graph is not a simple relationship. To begin with, as the pH increases, the time taken to digest the starch is shorter. After a certain point, the reaction starts to take longer again.

k What pH do you think will give the shortest time for amylase to digest starch? Explain your answer.

pH	Time taken to digest all the starch in seconds
2	Starch not digested
3	480
4	240
5	180
6	160
7	180
8	240
9	480
10	Starch not digested

Questions

1. Why do we use lines of best fit?

2. What is the difference between the relationships shown by straight-line graphs and those shown by curved-line graphs?

3. Sometimes the results do not all fit the pattern of the graph. Think about any experiments you have carried out in the past where the results were not what you expected. Why did this happen?

What makes a good fuel?

John, Clarissa and Dermont are discussing what makes an ideal fuel.

> It needs to give out a lot of thermal energy when it burns.

> It must be easy to set it alight.

> It shouldn't be toxic, and the fumes it gives off shouldn't be toxic.

> It mustn't be too flammable, or it will burst into flames before you want to use it.

> The less smoke it gives off, the better.

> When it burns it shouldn't make gases that pollute the air.

> It needs to be easy to transport.

> It depends what you want to use it for, and where you are living.

a Are petrol, coal and natural gas ideal fuels? Explain your answer.

Keep the home fires burning

Our homes used to be heated using fires. In Britain we used to burn wood on our fires. More recently we have burned coal and 'smokeless' fuel.

b What substance in the air is involved in all burning reactions?

c 'Smokeless' fuel is mainly carbon.
Write a word equation for burning carbon.

d Write an energy transfer diagram for a wood fire.

Other people around the world use different fuels to heat their homes. Inuits, who live in frozen wastelands, use blubber. Blubber is the layer of fat found under the skins of seals. The Bedouin people live in the desert. They use camel dung as fuel.

e Explain why neither the Inuits nor the Bedouin use wood as a fuel.

f Where did the energy in the camel dung come from? Draw an energy transfer diagram to explain your answer.

Fuels for vehicles

When fuels burn they react with another substance and the chemical reaction releases a lot of energy. Most common fuels, like petrol or diesel, react with oxygen from the air when they burn. However, there are situations when air is not available, for example high up in the atmosphere or in space. In these situations, you have to carry the oxygen in the vehicle. Burning is one type of **oxidation** reaction – we say the fuel is **oxidised**.

Questions

1. Look at this list of eight different vehicles. **E** to **H** are shown in the photos above.

   A car   **B** lorry   **C** steam engine   **D** jet plane   **E** 'top fuel' drag racer
   F V-2 rocket (used at the end of the Second World War)
   G Saturn V rocket (used to launch *Apollo* craft in 1960s and 1970s)
   H Space Shuttle with its solid fuel booster rockets

   The table below gives you information about eight different fuels.
   a Pair up each vehicle with its fuel. Write down the pairs.
   b Prepare a list of reasons for each choice, ready to join in a discussion.

Fuel	Reacts with	Notes
Nitromethane and methanol	Oxygen from the air	The energy is released in a sudden burst. The fuel burns very quickly.
Coal	Oxygen from the air	The fuel burns steadily.
Liquid hydrogen	Liquid oxygen	Liquid hydrogen and oxygen are expensive. They are kept in huge insulated tanks and pumped into the fuel tank as required. Liquid oxygen is easier, cheaper and safer to make than liquid hydrogen.
Petrol	Oxygen from the air	Petrol is available from petrol stations. It is easily pumped from one tank to another.
Diesel	Oxygen from the air	Diesel is available from petrol stations. It is cheaper than petrol. Diesel engines give poorer performance than petrol engines.
Ethanol (75%) and water (25%)	Liquid oxygen	Ethanol and water are easily available. Liquid oxygen can be made by cooling air until it turns into a liquid, then distilling it.
Kerosene	Oxygen from the air	Kerosene is more expensive than petrol. It gives out more energy per kilogram of fuel burned than petrol.
Powdered aluminium and polybutadiene-acrylonitrile-acrylic acid	Ammonium chlorate(VII)	Ammonium chlorate(VII) is used as a source of oxygen. Both the fuel and the ammonium chlorate(VII) are solids. The polybutadiene-acylonitrile-acrylic acid can be poured into the tanks as a liquid, then becomes a rubbery solid, holding the powdered aluminium and the ammonium chlorate(VII) together until the reaction is started.

What are fossil fuels?

We find **coal**, **oil** and **natural gas** inside rocks. All three are fuels because, when they are burned, they release lots of energy. They are called **fossil fuels** because they formed from animals and plants that lived millions of years ago. A fossil is the dead remains of an animal or plant preserved in rock.

Learn about

➤ The formation of coal, oil and natural gas

Why are fossil fuels important?

Our modern lifestyle needs a lot of energy, and most of this comes from fossil fuels. The petrol and diesel we use in cars and buses are made from crude oil. We burn oil, coal or natural gas for central heating in our homes. Most power stations in Britain burn coal, oil or natural gas to make the electricity we use at home.

As well as energy, we need many materials. We find some of these materials around us, but we have to make most of them. Materials we make are called **synthetic materials**. They include plastics and synthetic fabrics like polyester and nylon. Many synthetic materials are made from crude oil. Crude oil is a very versatile raw material. All the objects in the photo were made from crude oil.

a Give two reasons why fossil fuels are useful in our modern society.

How did fossil fuels form?

Usually, dead plants and animals are slowly changed into carbon dioxide, water and other oxides by bacteria. However, if the dead plants and animals are kept away from oxygen, then this normal rotting process does not happen.

Coal is made from plants that lived millions of years ago. They grew using energy from sunlight (1). When they died, the plants were buried (2). Instead of rotting, the plants changed, slowly, into coal. To make coal, plants were under pressure and heated to about 100 °C. The pressure was caused by the layers of mud and sediment on top of the plants (3). As the plants turned into coal, the layers of mud and sediment turned into rock (4). These processes took many millions of years.

b Write a 'recipe' for making coal.

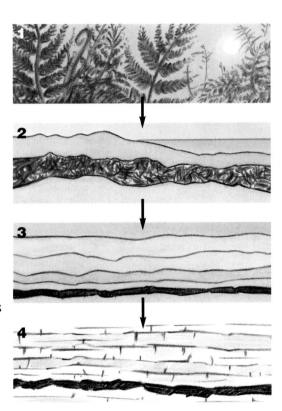

Oil and natural gas formed in a similar way, but they were made mostly from animals. Many millions of years ago, like now, the sea was full of tiny animals. These animals lived by eating plants, which made their food by trapping the energy in sunlight.

When these animals died they sank to the bottom of the sea where there was very little oxygen. Without oxygen, the tiny sea animals did not rot. Instead they were buried and put under pressure by layers of sediment forming above them. They were heated to about 100 °C. Slowly, over many millions of years, the dead sea animals changed into crude oil and natural gas while the sediments around them changed into rock.

Some rocks contain tiny holes. We say that these rocks are **porous**. Crude oil is a liquid and natural gas is, of course, a gas. The crude oil moved and collected in the porous rocks, like water in a sponge. The natural gas collected above the crude oil, in the tiny holes.

c Make a series of labelled drawings showing the formation of crude oil and natural gas.

What's in fossil fuels?

Coal, crude oil and natural gas are each mixtures of different substances. Many of the substances are hydrocarbons. Hydrocarbon molecules contain only carbon atoms and hydrogen atoms.

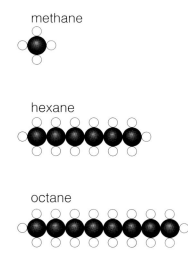

Natural gas contains a lot of **methane**. Each methane molecule has one carbon atom and four hydrogen atoms. The **formula** for methane is CH_4. The formula for a molecule is a 'shorthand' that tells us (a) which atoms are present and (b) how many of each atom. Crude oil contains many different hydrocarbons. Two others, hexane and octane, are shown in the diagram. A hexane molecule contains 6 carbon atoms and 14 hydrogen atoms, so its formula is C_6H_{14}. The formula for octane is C_8H_{18}. This tells us that there are 8 carbon atoms and 18 hydrogen atoms in one molecule of octane.

Questions

1. Write an energy transfer diagram to show how energy from the Sun was trapped in natural gas for millions of years and then released when the natural gas was burned.

2. Look at the diagram opposite.
   a What is the formula for a molecule of:
   i methane?   **ii** oxygen?
   iii carbon dioxide?   **iv** water?
   b The formula for hexane is C_6H_{14}
   How many molecules of:
   i carbon dioxide   **ii** water
   will form when one molecule of hexane is burned?

3. Imagine a carbon atom in a carbon dioxide molecule in the air 150 million years ago. It ends up back in the air as carbon dioxide when you use a Bunsen burner. Write a story called 'The Adventures of Calvin the Carbon Atom'.

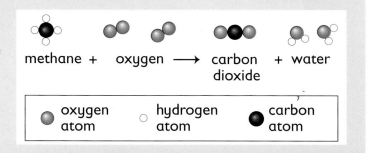

methane +   oxygen ⟶   carbon   + water
                          dioxide

| oxygen atom | hydrogen atom | carbon atom |

For your notes

The energy stored in fossil fuels came from the Sun.

Fossil fuels:

- include coal, crude oil and natural gas
- provide most of the energy we use and are important raw materials
- were made from buried animals and plants. This took many millions of years.

Releasing the energy

Natural gas is mostly methane which burns easily. Burning natural gas usually makes carbon dioxide and water, and releases a lot of thermal energy. A small amount of energy is also released as light energy.

Coal contains lots of different substances, including carbon and sulfur. These all react with the oxygen in the air when the coal is burned. Not all the carbon in the coal burns. Tiny bits of carbon are left. These make smoke.

Oil is different. When crude oil comes out of the ground it is a thick, sticky liquid that will not burn. The mixture in the crude oil needs to be separated. This is done by distillation. Many of the products of distillation make excellent fuels. These include butane (lighter fuel), petrol, kerosene (jet fuel), diesel and fuel oil.

Learn about

▶ Burning fossil fuels

energy stored in the...

natural gas

as **chemical energy**

energy transferred as ...
thermal energy

energy transferred as ...
light energy

a Write a word equation for burning:
  i carbon   **ii** sulfur
  when there is a lot of oxygen available.

b Butane is a hydrocarbon (chemical formula C_4H_{10}). What two substances will be produced when butane is burned?

Global warming

Carbon dioxide is made when we burn fossil fuels. Carbon dioxide in the air traps the Sun's energy in the atmosphere rather than it being lost into space. This is called the greenhouse effect.

Releasing more carbon dioxide into the atmosphere increases the greenhouse effect and this may be making the Earth hotter. This is called **global warming**.

Making the Earth hotter will change our environment. Some of the ice at the North and South Poles will melt, and the water in the seas and oceans will expand slightly. This will make the sea level rise, and land that is low will be flooded. Weather patterns will change – for example, the annual rainfall will increase in some places and decrease in others. Ocean currents may change. The Earth would become a very different place, both for us and for other living things.

c Would:
  i burning less fossil fuels
  ii cutting down trees
  increase or decrease the greenhouse effect?

  Explain your answers.

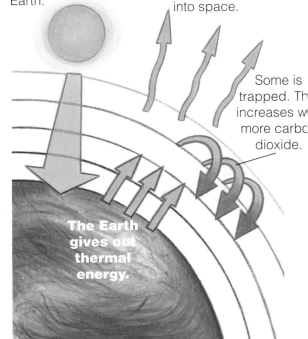

Energy from the Sun heats up the Earth.

Some escapes into space.

Some is trapped. Th increases w more carbo dioxide.

The Earth gives out thermal energy.

Air pollution

Burning coal releases a lot of sulfur dioxide, which can cause acid rain and other pollution problems. We now put chemical **scrubbers** in power station chimneys to remove the sulfur dioxide given out. These chemical scrubbers contain an alkali solution. The sulfur dioxide dissolves in the solution, making an acid which is neutralised by the alkali.

Vehicles pollute the air. They give out tiny bits of carbon (smoke), nitrogen oxides, carbon monoxide, unburned hydrocarbons and carbon dioxide. High levels of these pollutants cause health problems, particularly to people with asthma. On sunny days the problem is worse, because the pollutants react to produce other toxic substances, such as ozone.

Foggy, polluted air makes **smog**. Smog used to be caused by fog mixing with smoke from coal fires. The smog was reduced when burning coal in built-up areas was banned. Modern smog is usually caused by a mixture of fog and pollutants from cars and lorries.

Fitting cars with **catalytic converters** reduces air pollution. Catalytic converters change nitrogen oxides into nitrogen and carbon monoxide into carbon dioxide. In Britain, we test every car to check that it does not produce too many pollutants. Owners of cars with small engines, which make less pollution, pay less in car tax. Reducing the number of cars, by improving public transport and encouraging car sharing, also helps.

d The table shows three solutions. Which solution could be used as a chemical scrubber to remove sulfur dioxide from smoke? Explain your answer.

Solution	pH
Sodium chloride	7
Sodium chlorate	3
Sodium hydroxide	14

Did you know?

In 1952, over 4000 Londoners died because of very heavy smog.

e Do catalytic converters help reduce the greenhouse effect? Explain your answer.

Questions

1. Draw an energy transfer diagram for fuel oil burning.

2. Air pollution in Athens became so bad that half the cars were banned from driving into the city on any one day.
   a How would this decrease air pollution?
   b Do you think it was a good idea?
   c What other measures can be used to reduce the amount of air pollution produced by cars and lorries?

3. Imagine living in a low-lying coastal area of Britain in the year 2050. Global warming has increased the average temperature by 3 °C. The sea level has risen. A warm ocean current has changed direction, so the sea is much colder. The annual rainfall has decreased. How would life have changed for:
   a a fisherman?   **b** a farmer?
   c a family owning a hotel on the coast road?

For your notes

Thermal energy is released when fossil fuels are burned.

Carbon dioxide is made when fossil fuels are burned.

Increased amounts of carbon dioxide in the air may cause **global warming**.

Burning coal makes sulfur dioxide, which causes acid rain.

Unburned carbon from fuels makes smoke.

Electricity from fossil fuels

Inside a power station

Our electricity is made in power stations. Most of our power stations use fossil fuels as their source of energy. The fossil fuels are burned, and the energy released is transferred to electricity.

Water is heated in the boiler, and turned into steam. The steam takes up a lot more space than the water, so it rushes out of the boiler and into the **turbine**, like steam rushing out of the spout of a kettle. The steam turns the blades of the turbine. The spinning turbine turns the **generator**. When the generator turns it produces electricity.

Learn about

➤ How fossil fuels are used to make electricity

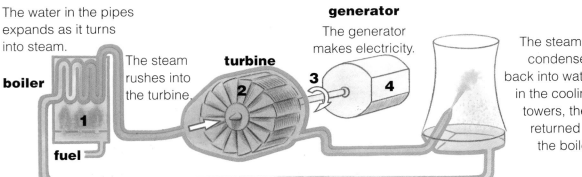

The water in the pipes expands as it turns into steam.

boiler

The steam rushes into the turbine.

turbine

generator
The generator makes electricity.

The steam is condensed back into water in the cooling towers, then returned to the boiler.

1

fuel

2

3

4

a Where does: **i** evaporation **ii** condensation take place in a power station?

Transferring the energy

1. The fossil fuels are burned, releasing thermal energy. This heats water and turns it into steam.

energy stored in ...

fossil fuels

as **chemical energy**

energy transferred as ... → steam
thermal energy

2. The turbine is turned by the jet of steam. Kinetic energy is transferred to the turbine by the steam.

steam *energy transferred as ...* → turbine
kinetic energy

3. The turbine spins the generator. Kinetic energy is transferred from the turbine to the generator.

turbine *energy transferred as ...* → generator
kinetic energy

4. The generator takes in kinetic energy and gives out electrical energy.

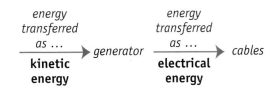

energy transferred as ... → generator *energy transferred as ...* → cables
kinetic energy   **electrical energy**

b What transfers the energy between the boiler and the turbine?

Wasted energy

Not all the energy released when the fuel burns ends up in the water. Some of it will be lost to the surroundings (**A**).

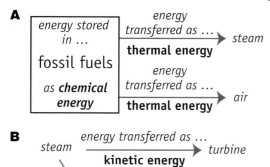

It is the kinetic energy of the steam that is transferred to the turbine. The thermal energy of the steam is not transferred. Much of this thermal energy will be lost to the surroundings when the steam is condensed back into water in the cooling towers (**B**).

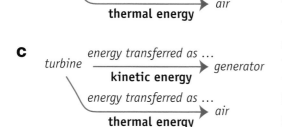

There will be friction in the turbine. Due to this friction, some of the kinetic energy of the turbine will end up as thermal energy, instead of being transferred to the generator (**C**).

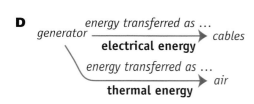

There will also be friction in the generator. Some of the kinetic energy of the generator will end up as thermal energy, rather than as electrical energy (**D**).

Only a small proportion of the energy released from the burning fuel ends up as electrical energy.

c Where does most of the 'wasted' energy end up?

d Does the 'wasted' energy end up as electrical energy, kinetic energy or thermal energy?

The future

The problem with fossil fuels is that they are going to run out. Fossil fuels are **non-renewable** energy resources. The fossil fuels took many millions of years to form. They are not being replaced as fast as we use them.

It is difficult to decide how soon we will run out of fossil fuels. It depends on how fast we use them, and it depends on whether we find more oil fields and coal deposits. Scientists suggest we will run out of oil in about 2030, natural gas in about 2050 and coal in about 2230. That means no petrol for vehicles after 2030. It means that we will have to convert all our oil and natural gas power stations to burn coal instead over the next 50 years. That will only put off the problem, and we will use up the coal sooner. At the moment, 90% of our energy comes from fossil fuels. We need to find other ways to get the energy we need. We are going to have to find some **alternative** energy resources.

Questions

1. Use the information on these pages to draw an energy transfer diagram that shows all the energy transfers in a power station. You will need a large piece of paper. Show the 'wanted' energy transfers in one colour and the 'unwanted' ones in another.

2. **a** How many years before we use up all the:
   i coal? **ii** natural gas? **iii** oil?
   b What will happen to the price of fossil fuels as they run out?

3. Imagine life in 100 years' time when all the natural gas and oil has run out and coal is rare and expensive. Make a list of the changes that will have taken place.

For your notes

Power stations change the chemical energy stored in fuels into electrical energy.

Only a small part of the energy in the fuel ends up as electrical energy.

Non-renewable energy resources (such as fossil fuels) are not replaced as fast as we use them.

Turning the turbine

Biomass

Methane can be used as a fuel. We find methane in natural gas, but methane can also be made from rotting plants and animals. The tank in the photo contains farm waste, being used to make methane. This methane is an example of **biomass**. Biomass is material from plants and animals that can be used as an energy resource. Wood is another example of biomass.

The energy stored in the biomass comes from the Sun. The trees trap the energy from sunlight and use it to make wood. Rubbish is material from plants and animals. The animals eat plants, or other animals that eat plants, so their energy comes from the Sun.

Unlike fossil fuels, wood and methane are **renewable** sources of energy. A tree only takes 10–15 years to grow. We produce a lot of rubbish that can be rotted to make methane.

These fuels can be used in the boiler of a power station. Energy will be transferred to the steam, which will turn the turbine. The turbine turns the generator, producing electricity.

(a) Explain why wood is a renewable energy resource, while coal is not.

Solar energy

It is also possible to turn water into steam using energy directly from the Sun. **Solar furnaces** are huge, curved mirrors that reflect all the sunlight to a single point. This concentrates the thermal energy from the Sun, so that it is intense enough to turn water into steam. The steam is then used to turn the turbine in the usual way.

Solar furnaces are very expensive to build. It would not be worth building a solar furnace in a region that often had cloudy skies. It is best to build solar furnaces near the equator. This is because the energy from the Sun is less spread over the Earth's surface near the equator, and has to go through less atmosphere. This is shown on the diagram.

Solar energy is renewable – the Sun renews it continuously.

(b) In Britain, we sometimes use solar energy to heat water to use in our homes, but we do not build solar furnaces. Explain why.

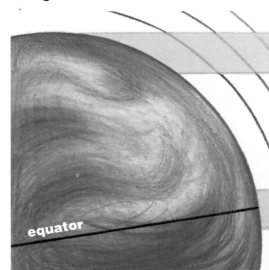

Further north, the sunlight goes through more atmosphere and is spread out more when it hits the surface.

At the equator, the sunlight goes through less atmosphere and is more concentrated when it hits the surface.

equator

Wind energy

Instead of heating water and turning it into steam, you can turn the turbine directly. **Wind turbines** are turned by **wind energy**. The turbine turns the generator, and electricity is made.

$$Sun \xrightarrow[\textbf{thermal energy}]{energy\ transferred\ as\ ...} air \xrightarrow[\textbf{kinetic energy}]{energy\ transferred\ as\ ...} turbine$$

Winds are caused by the Sun. Thermal energy from the Sun heats some parts of the atmosphere more than others. Where the atmosphere is heated more, the air becomes less dense and rises. Cooler air rushes in to take the place of the rising air. The moving air is wind. The Sun heats the atmosphere every day, so wind is a renewable energy resource.

Some houses or businesses have a single wind turbine to provide the electricity they need. Large collections of wind turbines are called **wind farms**. The electricity from a wind farm, along with the electricity from power stations, is available for all electricity consumers to use. Many people think wind farms are ugly, and they can be noisy.

c Where would you build a wind farm? Give your reasons.

Waves

Wave energy can also be used to turn the turbine. One way of doing this is shown in the diagram. When a wave hits, the water level in the chamber rises. This forces air out of the chamber and through the turbine. This turns the turbine, which spins the generator.

Waves are made by wind passing over the water. As wind is a renewable energy resource, so are waves.

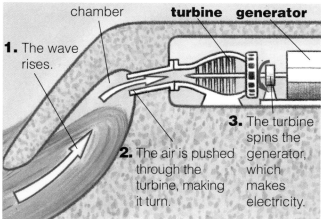

chamber   **turbine**   **generator**

1. The wave rises.

2. The air is pushed through the turbine, making it turn.

3. The turbine spins the generator, which makes electricity.

Questions

1. The alternative energy resources shown on these two pages are renewable.
   a What does 'renewable' mean?
   b Why is it important to develop renewable energy resources?

2. Draw energy transfer diagrams showing how the Sun's energy is used to generate electricity using:
   a a solar furnace   **b** a wave generator.

3. Even alternative energy resources affect the environment. Discuss the impact on the environment of:
   a a biomass power station   **b** a wind farm.

For your notes

Biomass, solar power, wind and **waves**:

- are energy resources
- can be used to generate electricity
- are renewable
- get their energy from the Sun.

Renewable energy resources are replaced as we use them.

Learn about

➤ More alternative energy resources

Hydroelectric power

We use falling water to generate electricity. The water falls through the turbine, turning it. The turbine then turns the generator. This is called **hydroelectric** power.

Waterfalls can turn turbines. Some of these waterfalls are natural but many have been built. The photo shows the Hoover Dam, built across the Colorado River in the USA. There is a huge artificial lake behind the dam. Water from the lake falls through the turbines, generating electricity.

The water in rivers comes from rain. The water in the rain has been lifted up when water was evaporated by the Sun. Water is evaporated each day, so falling water is a renewable energy resource.

Hydroelectric power stations are expensive to build but the running costs are low. A hydroelectric power station produces very little pollution. However, modifying a waterfall changes the flow of the river, and building a dam usually makes a huge lake. Habitats are destroyed and many animals and plants are killed.

a Copy and complete this energy transfer diagram showing how energy from the Sun is used to turn the turbines in the Hoover Dam.

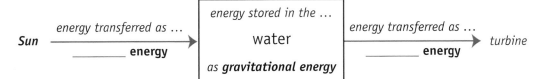

Sun → *energy transferred as ...* _____ **energy** → energy stored in the ... water as *gravitational energy* → *energy transferred as ...* _____ **energy** → turbine

Tides

Tides can also be used to lift water up to make a store of gravitational energy. A barrier is built. This can be a dam, like the one across the Rance River near Saint-Malo in Brittany. At high tide, the water is allowed to flow through the dam. The dam is then closed and the tide goes out. Now there is a height difference between the two sides, and water is allowed to fall through turbines.

Tides are not caused by thermal energy from the Sun. They are caused by gravity. The Moon and the Sun pull on the Earth, moving the water in the oceans. This pull is continuous, so tides are a renewable energy resource.

Again, building a barrage or a dam is very expensive but the running costs are cheap and there is very little pollution. The dam or barrage will change habitats, and some animals and plants will die.

Nuclear and geothermal energy

Some elements such as uranium are **radioactive**. Their atoms break down, giving out lots of energy. At a **nuclear** power station, this energy is transferred into electrical energy. Radioactive material is kept sealed up. The thermal energy given out by the core is used to heat water and turn it into steam. The steam then turns the turbine.

Nuclear power stations are expensive to build. They are cheap to run but very expensive to take apart when they are too old to work properly. If safety precautions are not taken, there is a small chance that the radioactive core will give out too much energy too quickly and cause an explosion. This happened at Chernobyl in 1986. This type of explosion puts radioactive atoms into the air, which can kill or cause cancer. The photo shows the exploded power station at Chernobyl. It was encased in concrete to stop more radioactive atoms escaping.

The inside of the Earth is hot. This is partly because the Earth was very hot when it formed and is still cooling down, and partly because the Earth contains radioactive elements, like uranium. These elements are breaking down and releasing energy. In some places there are hot rocks quite close to the surface. If you pump cold water down to these rocks, it returns as steam. This can be used to turn a turbine in a **geothermal** power station. These power stations are expensive to build but cheap to run. They produce very little pollution. However, there are very few places with the right type of hot rocks to build a geothermal power station.

The radioactive atoms that break down and give out energy in a nuclear or geothermal power station are not replaced. However, supplies of radioactive substances will last a very long time.

The energy given out when radioactive atoms break down does not come from our Sun. Like all atoms, the radioactive atoms were made in other stars and then scattered across the galaxy when those stars exploded. When the Solar System formed, some of these atoms came together to make the Earth.

b Do you think nuclear energy and geothermal energy are renewable?

Questions

1. **a** Make a list of all the energy resources you have learned about.
   b Divide the energy resources into two groups, 'renewable' and 'non-renewable'.
   c Divide the energy resources into two new groups, those that get their energy from the Sun and those that get their energy from radioactive elements or gravity.

2. Use the information on pages 82–7 and your general knowledge to think of one advantage and one disadvantage of each energy resource below. You cannot use any advantage or disadvantage more than once.

   coal   oil   natural gas   wind   waves
   nuclear power   falling water
   geothermal power   biomass   solar power

For your notes

Falling water is a renewable energy resource that can be used to generate electricity. This is called **hydroelectric power**.

The energy in falling river water comes from the Sun.

Tides can be used to make electricity. Tides are caused by gravity, not thermal energy from the Sun.

Nuclear and **geothermal** power are two other energy resources.

Learn about

➤ Transport of the future

Life without oil

Our lifestyle is very dependent on transport. We often travel by car or bus. The clothes we wear, the food we eat and the goods we buy are all transported by road or sea or air. Cars, ships and planes all need fuel, which is made from oil. But the oil is going to run out by 2030. There will be no petrol or diesel, and no kerosene for the planes.

Conserving energy

To try to make the oil last longer, we could stop burning oil in power stations, and generate our electricity using other energy resources. We could make cars with smaller engines which burn less petrol and give us more miles to the gallon (or kilometres to the litre). The Government is encouraging us to do this by charging less tax for cars with small engines. However, this will only put off the inevitable. We will run out of oil.

Alternative fuels

Countries in South America only have a small amount of oil. They have to buy their oil from other countries, which puts them at a disadvantage. Brazil, the largest country in South America, grows a lot of sugar cane but has very little oil. The Brazilians decided to make an alternative fuel from sugar. They fermented the sugar to make ethanol. They then used the ethanol in their cars rather than petrol.

Hydrogen may be an alternative fuel for the future. Hydrogen is a very clean fuel, which releases a lot of energy when it burns. There are two problems with hydrogen – it is a gas and it explodes.

One solution is to carry the hydrogen as a hydrogen compound rather than hydrogen gas. The hydrogen would be released from the compound in a chemical reaction, just before it was needed.

(a) Ethanol has the formula C_2H_6O. What two compounds will be formed when ethanol reacts with oxygen?

(b) Write a word equation for the reaction of hydrogen and oxygen.

(c) Why, from an environmental point of view, is hydrogen a better fuel than ethanol?

Batteries

Another alternative to petrol is electric cars powered by **batteries**. We have had electric cars for years. Milk floats are powered by batteries. However, electric cars have never caught on. Batteries were very heavy and, even when fully charged, could only provide enough energy to travel short distances slowly.

energy stored in the ...		
batteries	*energy transferred as ...* **electrical energy** → motor	*energy transferred as ...* **kinetic energy** →
as **chemical energy**		

The technology has improved. Modern batteries are lighter and can store more energy than the older type. Modern electric cars are made of lightweight materials, so less energy is needed for them to go fast. The very best electric cars accelerate like a petrol car and can travel long distances before the batteries need charging. However, these cars are very expensive and the batteries take up a lot of room, often the whole of the boot or the whole of the back seat.

Solar powered cars

Solar cells can be used to make electricity. Sunlight falls on the solar cell and it produces electricity. The Solar Challenge is a race across Australia held every year, for cars powered by solar cells. However, the cars are not very practical. The solar cells are very expensive and they cover a big surface on top of the car. The car cannot carry much weight, just the driver. Also, the race is held in Australia because solar cars need a lot of sunlight!

Fuel cells

Fuel cells take the energy given out in a chemical reaction and turn it into electrical energy:

energy stored in ...	energy transferred as ...
hydrogen and oxygen	electrical energy
as **chemical energy**	

Fuel cells are not a new idea. There were fuel cells on the *Apollo* spacecraft used for the Moon missions of the 1960s. These early fuel cells were dangerous because they were based on the reaction between hydrogen and oxygen, which is explosive. Modern fuel cells, like the ones in the fuel cell power station in the photo, are much safer, but they are still very expensive. A big advantage of fuel cells is that they are very efficient. Almost all the energy released in the chemical reaction ends up as electrical energy.

Questions

1. Write an energy transfer diagram for a solar cell.

2. What are the advantages and disadvantages of hydrogen as a fuel?

3. Why have battery cars failed to catch on?

4. Could you use a solar powered car, like the ones used in the Solar Challenge, as a family car in Britain? Give as many reasons as you can for your answer.

5. Which energy resource will power the cars of the future? Give your reasons.

For your notes

Batteries store chemical energy and convert it into electrical energy.

Solar cells convert light energy into electrical energy.

Fuel cells convert the energy released in chemical reactions into electrical energy.

How many?

Energy resources

6.8

Counting wild animals

Ed, Lonnie and Catherine have been watching a programme about a group of scientists who are studying snails. The scientists wanted to know how many snails were living in a meadow. They **sampled** the snails. The flow chart shows how they did this. From their samples they **estimated** the number of snails in the meadow (the population).

10 of the snails in the second sample had paint on their shells. The scientists used ratios to estimate how many snails were in the meadow. They calculated that there were 500 snails. The ratio of 'painted snails recaptured':'all snails painted' is the same as the ratio of 'size of second sample':'population'.

Snails painted = 100

Painted snails recaptured = 10

'Painted snails recaptured':'all snails painted' = 10:100 = 1:10

This means there are always 10 snails in the meadow for every 1 snail caught.

So when they caught 50 snails, they calculated that there were 50 × 10 = 500 snails in the meadow. The population of snails was 500.

You can write it like this:

10:100 = 1:10 = 50:?   ? = 500

Think about

▶ Sampling

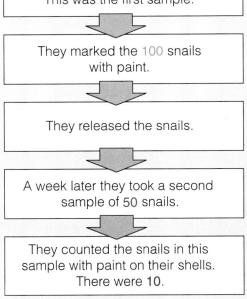

They caught 100 snails in traps. This was the first sample.

They marked the 100 snails with paint.

They released the snails.

A week later they took a second sample of 50 snails.

They counted the snails in this sample with paint on their shells. There were 10.

a What was the ratio of 'painted snails recaptured':'all snails painted'?

b What was the ratio of 'size of second sample':'population'?

c In an experiment in another meadow, there were only 5 marked snails out of 50 in the second sample.
  i What was the ratio of 'painted snails recaptured':'all snails painted'?
  ii What was the ratio of 'size of second sample':'population'?
  iii How many snails were in the second meadow?

Studying pollution

A group of scientists were studying pollution in a country where many new coal-fired power stations were being built. They studied two sites where new power stations were being built, and two sites with no power station. All the power stations were built by lakes, because a power station needs lots of water. The scientists decided to study pollution by looking at a type of fish in the lakes.

90

They caught 500 fish.

⬇

They put paint on each fish.

⬇

They released the fish.

⬇

One month later they took a second sample of 100 fish.

⬇

They counted the number of fish with paint.

⬇

They used ratios to estimate the population of fish.

Sampling problems

Ed, Lonnie and Catherine were discussing what could have gone wrong with the snail sampling experiment. They made these points.

- *The paint could make the snails more visible to predators.*
- *The snails could be poisoned by the paint.*
- *The shape of the trap may mean you only catch small snails.*
- *The painted snails may not mix up with the rest of the snails in one week.*
- *There could be places in the meadow where few snails go, or where lots of snails go.*

The scientists sampled the fish at each site every two years for ten years. They used different paint each time. The flow chart shows what they did. Their results are summarised in the table below.

d Copy the table. Find the missing populations.

e Make a bar chart for each site. Put the year along the bottom and the estimated population up the side.

f Does building a power station affect the population of this type of fish? Use the scientists' results in your answer.

g What effect would each of these problems have on the experiment?

h What problems could have occurred with the scientists' research into pollution?

Code: fish marked with paint = 500   number of painted fish caught again   sample size = 100   population

☐ without power station   ▨ with power station

Site	1988	1990	1992	1994	1996
1	5 5:500 = 1:100 = 100:? ? = 10000	5 5:500 = 1:100 = 100:? ? = 10000	5 5:500 = 1:100 = 100:? ? = 10000	5 5:500 = 1:100 = 100:? ? = 10000	5 5:500 = 1:100 = 100:? ? = 10000
2	5 5:500 = 1:100 = 100:? ? = 10000	5 5:500 = 1:100 = 100:? ? = 10000	25 25:500 = 1:20 = 100:? ? = 2000	50 50:500 = 1:10 = 100:? ? = 1000	50 50:500 = 1:10 = 100:? ? = 1000
3	6	5	7	6	4
4	5	23	36	48	39

Questions

Think about the scientists' pollution research.

1. Why did the scientists study two sites without power stations?

2. Suggest two things *other than* pollution that could change the population of fish.

3. The scientists concluded that coal-burning power stations make lake water acidic, which kills fish. What additional experiments should the scientists do to check their conclusion?

The fossil finder

Mary Anning is thought by many people to be the greatest fossil hunter the world ever knew. She did a lot of work to further our understanding of dinosaurs. Mary was born in Lyme Regis, Dorset in 1799. Her father died when she was just 11, leaving the family with no source of income.

To make money for her family, Mary began to collect fossils from the local beach. She would then sell them to wealthy collectors and museums. Fossil hunting was a dangerous business as it involved walking and wading under crumbling cliffs at low tide.

She gained quite a reputation as a fossil hunter and she made some very important discoveries. Mary found the first specimen of an *Ichthyosaurus* in 1821 and the first nearly complete fossilised skeleton of a *Plesiosaurus* in 1823. She found many other types of dinosaur as well.

Mary Anning.

Did you know?

The word 'dinosaur' means 'terrible lizard' in Greek. *Deinos* = terrible and *sauros* = lizard.

Ichthyosaurus.

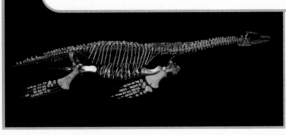

Plesiosaurus.

What are fossils?

Fossils are any parts of animals or plants that are preserved in rocks. The dead animals and plants become covered by layers of earth that turn into rocks over millions of years. Fossils are very important because they can tell us about organisms that existed millions of years ago. Much of our knowledge of the ancient world comes from fossils. Being a palaeontologist is a bit like being a detective.

Bones, shells and teeth are the best known fossils. But fossils can also be found of many other things, such as footprints, tiny seeds and animal dung. Whether animals and plants become fossilised depends on the conditions around them when they die.

(a) Why do you think that hard parts of an animal, like bones and shells, are often fossilised, but soft parts like skin and muscle are not?

Did you know?

People who study fossils are called palaeontologists. *Palaeo* is Greek for prehistoric.

Rock history

Fossils can tell us the story of events that happened on the Earth hundreds, thousands or millions of years ago. Time so long ago is called **geological time**. A **geologist** is a scientist who studies rocks and the Earth.

Look at the photo of the Grand Canyon in Arizona, USA. It was carved out by a river. Near the top of the canyon the rocks are 100 million years old. At the very bottom they are almost one billion years old.

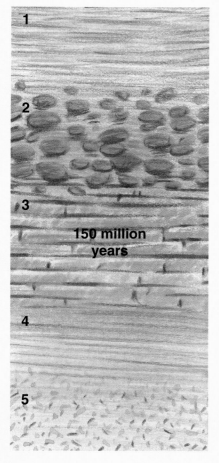

1
2
3
150 million years
4
5

If you dig down into the Earth and find a column of rock, you will find layers of different rocks. Different rocks are made in different ways.

If the rocks have not been disturbed, the rocks at the bottom will be the oldest. The rocks then go up in order of age. The youngest rock is at the top.

b Why will the oldest rocks be furthest down?

If a palaeontologist finds a fossil of an animal that we know only lived during a certain period of time, then we can tell that the rock that the fossil was found in was from that period. This works the other way too – if we know the age of the rock it is possible to work out the age of the fossil.

c A rock contains a fossil of an animal that lived between 70 and 85 million years ago. What is the oldest age that the rock could be?

Dinosaurs

Using fossil evidence, it can be shown that the first dinosaurs were on Earth about 200 million years ago. The last dinosaurs died out suddenly about 65 million years ago. Some scientists believe that the reason they died out so suddenly was because a very large meteorite or comet crashed into the Earth. Scientists are still collecting evidence about this.

It takes careful detective work to reassemble the fossilised bones of a dinosaur into a complete skeleton.

d You are putting together the bones of a dinosaur and one is missing. How will you decide what it was?

Questions

1. Answer the following questions using the diagram above.
   a Which layer of rock is the oldest?
   b Which layer of rock is the youngest?
   c Which is the most likely layer of rock to contain fossils of dinosaurs?
   d Which layers are older than 150 million years old?
   e Sometimes columns of rocks are turned upside down or on their side. Can you imagine what might happen to do this?

2. How are the dinosaurs thought to have become extinct? Why do we not know exactly?

3. Rocks older than 200 million years do not have dinosaur fossils in them. Why not?

4. Make up a poem about being an Earth detective. Try and use the following words:

fossils   dinosaur   geology   Earth

Rock breaking

Rocks and minerals

There are many types of rock, each type made up from different elements and compounds called **minerals**. There are more than 2000 known minerals, but most rocks are made from just 12 of them.

Rain and ice

Look at the photo. The bits of rock at the bottom of the slope used to be part of the mountain. They have been broken off the side of the mountain and then worn away into smaller chunks. This is called **weathering**. Rocks can fall at any time without warning, making it dangerous for mountaineers in the area.

When rock is broken into smaller pieces, but not changed into different substances, we call this **physical weathering**. This can be caused by the effect of wind, water and changes in temperature. This is a physical change – no new substances are formed.

Water expands when it freezes. You may know that if the water in house pipes freezes, it will expand and burst the pipes. Most rocks have a lot of small cracks. Water flows into the cracks. Some rocks are **porous**, which means they have tiny holes like a sponge. Water can also be absorbed into the holes in these rocks.

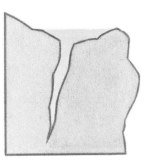

1. Water gets into cracks in the rock.

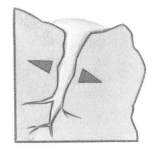

2. The water freezes and it expands.

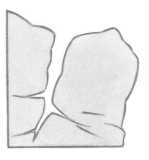

3. The force of the ice makes the crack bigger.

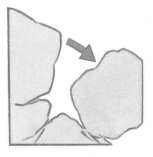

4. Eventually the crack gets so big that part of the rock breaks off.

When this water freezes, it expands and makes cracks bigger. Later, the ice thaws and more water gets into these larger cracks and freezes again. This makes the cracks even bigger. Eventually, the rock breaks apart. This process is known as **freeze-thaw**.

Potholes in a road are a good example of weathering caused by freeze-thaw.

a Explain how water can break a big rock into small chunks. Use the word 'ice' in your explanation.

b Explain why potholes in roads tend to get bigger in the winter.

Water

Rivers can carry large amounts of rock away from mountains and hills. The size of rock fragments that the river can carry depends on the speed of the water. Rivers move very fast near to their source in the mountain. Here the water can transport quite large fragments of rock. Rivers move more slowly when they get close to the sea and so they can only carry small grains of rock. As the photo of the house shows, the sea can also carry weathered material away.

b Would erosion be quicker near the source of a river or near where it reaches the sea? Explain your answer.

Deposition

As a river slows down, it can no longer carry along large pieces of rock. They settle to the bottom of the river. This is called **deposition**. Finally the river is travelling so slowly that only very fine grains of rock can still be carried along. The fine bits that settle out are called **sediment**.

The wide river mouth where a slow-moving river flows into the sea is called an **estuary**. Layers of sediment build up here to form new land, and the river runs over it in lots of small streams. This is called a **delta**.

c Why do you get a lot of sediment at the mouth of a river but not near its source?

river carrying sediment

delta

deposited sediment forms new land

sea

Questions

1. Flash floods happen when it rains very heavily in a short time in mountainous areas. The water cannot be absorbed into the soil, but runs off on the surface. Suggest what sort of effect a flash flood might have on the land.

2. In the diagram, sand is building up on the inside of the bend but not on the outside of the bend. What does this tell you about the speed of the water in the two parts of the bend? Explain your answer.

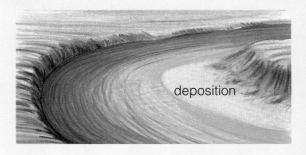

deposition

3. The port of Eureka is at the mouth of a very slow-moving river. It has to be dredged regularly to prevent the sediment getting too deep and stopping ships from passing though. Explain why the sediment builds up.

4. Explain how grains of granite can be found in the sediment at the mouth of River X, even though there are no granite rocks for miles.

For your notes

Erosion happens when rock is **transported** away from where it was weathered. Erosion wears away the rock pieces and makes them rounded.

Rock can be eroded by wind, water or **glaciers**.

Fast-moving wind and water can carry larger pieces of rock than slow-moving wind or water.

Deposition happens when pieces of rock that were transported settle again on to the Earth's surface.

99

Making rocks

The rock cycle

There are three main types of rock, and they change from one type to another over millions of years. This is called the **rock cycle**.

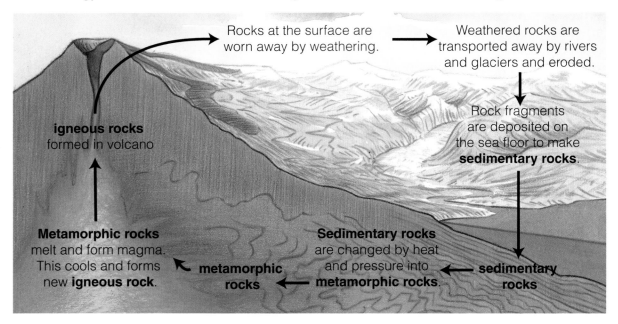

Rocks at the surface are worn away by weathering.

Weathered rocks are transported away by rivers and glaciers and eroded.

Rock fragments are deposited on the sea floor to make **sedimentary rocks**.

igneous rocks formed in volcano

Metamorphic rocks melt and form magma. This cools and forms new **igneous rock**.

metamorphic rocks

Sedimentary rocks are changed by heat and pressure into **metamorphic rocks**.

sedimentary rocks

Igneous rocks

Igneous rocks are formed out of molten rock or **magma** from deep within the Earth. The magma is pushed up to the top layer or **crust** of the Earth. When the magma reaches the surface it is called **lava**. Sometimes the magma is forced out and **erupts** from a volcano, as shown in the photo below.

Once it reaches the surface, the lava cools quickly and forms **extrusive igneous rock**. 'Extrusive' means 'on the surface'. The rock has small crystals. **Basalt** is an example of this sort of rock. Ocean floors are often made of basalt.

Sometimes the magma never reaches the surface but cools slowly underground between layers of rock. Rock formed like this is called **intrusive igneous rock**. 'Intrusive' means 'in between'. The rock has large crystals. **Granite** is an example of this sort of rock. Weathering or movements of the Earth's crust eventually bring these rocks to the surface.

ⓐ Why do you think lava on the surface cools more quickly than magma underground?

Sedimentary rocks

Sedimentary rocks are formed from sediments. The sediments are made up of small pieces called **grains** of rock, and shells of dead organisms. Deposits of sediment build up in layers over millions of years at the bottoms of lakes or seas. The photo below shows the layered structure of sedimentary rocks.

The pressure of the layers building up squeezes water out of the sediments at the bottom and squashes them together more tightly. Often there are chemicals dissolved in the water where sediments are deposited.

As the water is squeezed out and dries up, the chemicals can form crystals between the sediments to **cement** them together. Sedimentary rocks such as **limestone**, **mudstone** and **sandstone** are formed in this way. Another very useful sedimentary rock is coal, which is made from trees and ferns that were once living. Different particles make up different sedimentary rocks.

b Sedimentary rocks often have fossils in them. Why do you think this is?

Metamorphic rock

Metamorphic rock is formed when existing rocks are changed by heat or high pressure. As the rocks become buried deeper in the Earth, or are squeezed by earth movements, the temperature and pressure become higher. This causes the minerals to change chemically without the rocks actually melting. New minerals are formed. When new minerals form under pressure, their crystals line up in layers. **Slate** is an example of a metamorphic rock.

c When lava flows over the surface of a sediment, it is hot enough to bake it. Metamorphic rock formed like this does not have layers of crystals in it. Explain why not.

Completing the cycle

If metamorphic rocks become buried very deep, eventually the temperature becomes so high that the rocks melt and turn to magma again.

Questions

1. Write the following parts of the rock cycle in the correct order:

> **rocks melt   weathering   deposition   erosion
> sedimentary rocks form   volcanic eruption
> burying and squeezing**

2. You could use a sandwich as a model for the formation of sedimentary rocks. What could you do to the sandwich to model the metamorphic process? Can you think of something to model igneous rock formation?

W – particles of rock washed into the sea
X – rock heated and squeezed
Y – molten rock cooling slowly
Z – molten rock cooling quickly

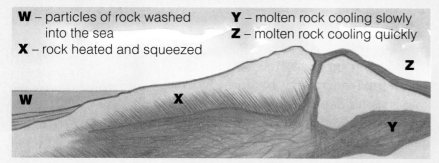

3. Look at the diagram above and then answer the questions.
   a At which place on the diagram would you expect the following rocks to be formed?
   i an igneous rock with small crystals
   ii an igneous rock with big crystals
   iii a metamorphic rock
   iv a sedimentary rock
   b Name one example of each of the rocks above.

Did you know?

The word 'metamorphic' comes from a Greek word meaning a change of form. 'Igneous' comes from the Greek word for fire.

4. As well as being buried by earth movements, sedimentary rocks can also be uplifted by earth movements such as earthquakes. Shale containing fossil sea shells is sometimes found on the tops of mountains. Explain in terms of the rock cycle how this is possible.

For your notes

The three main types of rock, **igneous**, **sedimentary** and **metamorphic**, are made in different ways.

They change from one type to another over millions of years.

These changes are summarised in the **rock cycle**.

101

Rock types

What are rocks?

Rocks are found everywhere. We walk on them and build with them. All rocks are made up of minerals. Different rocks are made up of different minerals or different mixtures of minerals. Granite is made up from three minerals – quartz, feldspar and mica.

Learn about

➤ Minerals

➤ Types of rock

Diamond.

Talc.

How hard? How dense?

The hardness of a mineral can be measured by using the **Mohs scale**. This is a number scale from 1 to 10. A mineral that is very soft such as talc is 1 on the scale, and one that is very hard such as diamond is 10. A fingernail is 3 on the scale.

a You cannot scratch a diamond with your fingernail, but you can scratch talc. Explain this.

Rocks also vary in their density. This depends on the minerals they contain. Minerals containing metals such as iron or magnesium are more dense than minerals containing non-metals such as silicon. The density also depends on how closely packed the atoms are in the mineral.

Did you know?

You can test rocks with hydrochloric acid to see if they contain calcium carbonate. The acid reacts with the calcium carbonate and fizzes to produce carbon dioxide.

Rock types

Geologists classify rocks into the three main types – **igneous**, **sedimentary** and **metamorphic**. As well as being formed in different ways, they have some very different properties.

Igneous rocks

These rocks are very hard and made up of crystals. We say they are **crystalline**. These rocks form from molten rock which cools and solidifies. The size of the crystals depends on how quickly or slowly the rock cooled. Basalt cools quickly and has crystals that are too small to see. Granite cools slowly and has big crystals.

Basalt.

Basalt and granite contain different amounts of silicate and iron. This means that they have different densities.

Basalt is a black rock. Granite looks mottled as it is made up of three different coloured minerals.

Igneous rocks do not fizz with hydrochloric acid. Igneous rocks are used for building and for road surfaces.

b A geologist found an igneous rock that has small crystals. Did it cool above or below ground? Explain your answer.

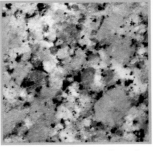

Granite.

Sedimentary rocks

Sedimentary rocks are made up of grains of other rocks or the remains of organisms. The rocks are made up of layers and sometimes contain fossils. Limestone is made from very small particles of calcium carbonate, which came from the shells of small sea animals. Millions of years ago there were warm shallow seas full of these sea animals, and limestone formed underneath them. **Chalk** is another example of a sedimentary rock. This is also made from calcium carbonate. Limestone and chalk fizz with hydrochloric acid. Sandstone is made from larger particles of sand and silicate. Most sedimentary rocks are less dense than igneous rocks.

Limestone is a very useful rock. As well as being used for building roads and houses it is also found in toothpaste and make-up. It is even added to bread as a source of calcium!

Metamorphic rocks

Metamorphic rocks are hard and are made of small crystals, often arranged in layers. Slate and **marble** are examples of metamorphic rocks. Slate comes from a sedimentary rock called **shale**. The shale is compressed and it changes to make slate.

Marble comes from limestone. The limestone is heated and compressed and changed into marble. Marble usually looks white or grey but sometimes has coloured patches in it. Slate does not react with acid, but marble does.

Slate is used to make roofs. Marble is often used as a building material or for sculptures.

Limestone.

Sandstone.

Slate.

Marble.

c A metamorphic rock made from a sedimentary rock will not have any fossils in it. Why do you think this is?

Questions

1. In what types of rock do you normally find fossils?

2. What is the Mohs scale?

3. For each rock type below, give one example and explain two ways that we could use it.
   a sedimentary   **b** metamorphic   **c** igneous

4. Use the information on these two pages to make a table about the properties of the following types of rocks: slate, marble, granite, basalt, limestone, sandstone.

5. **a** Give two properties that both granite and basalt have in common.
   b Give two properties that are different in granite and basalt.
   c Explain how these different properties came about.

For your notes

Rocks can be classified according to their properties, such as grain or crystal size, hardness, colour, density and chemical reactions.

Igneous rocks are very hard and are made up of crystals.

Sedimentary rocks are made up of grains in layers, and often have fossils in them.

Metamorphic rocks are hard and are often made of crystals arranged in layers.

Name that rock

Why and what?

These words are all question words. Questions are very important in science:

Why? What? How? Which? Where?

● Scientists carry out investigations to find out the answers to questions. It is important to ask the right kinds of questions if you want to find out anything useful.

● Scientists use questions when they are classifying things and putting them into groups. A key is a set of questions that helps us to classify things.

Out in the field

Class 8T are on a geology field trip. They are examining the rocks around them and testing them with acid. They are collecting small samples of different rocks to take back to the classroom. There they will find out about the properties of each rock, so they can look up in a reference book what sort of rock it is. This will also tell them how it was formed and help them discover how the landscape around them was made.

a To help the class identify the rocks back at the classroom, write a list of the questions they will need to ask and answer about each sample.

b In your group, look at all the questions you have written down. Decide which questions will be the most useful when identifying rocks.

c Is there something that all the useful questions have in common?

Identifying the rocks

Look at these photos of the rocks Hassan's group brought back.

d Use your questions to help you to identify each of the three rocks.

Back at the classroom, Lisa's group found they hadn't kept careful enough notes about their samples. To make matters worse, Lisa had felt ill by the end of the field trip and had gone straight home and taken the rock samples with her. The rest of the group put together the notes they had. These are shown on the next page.

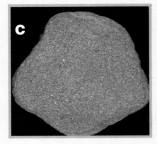

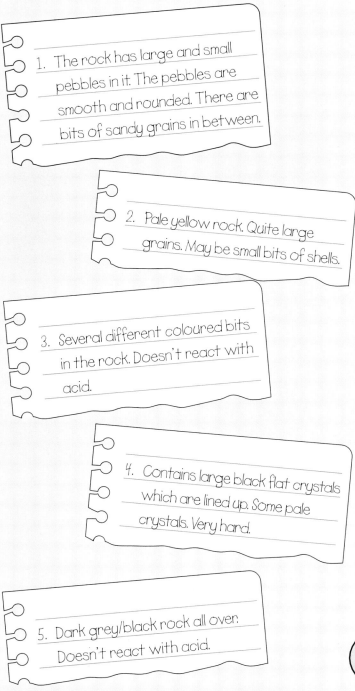

1. The rock has large and small pebbles in it. The pebbles are smooth and rounded. There are bits of sandy grains in between.

2. Pale yellow rock. Quite large grains. May be small bits of shells.

3. Several different coloured bits in the rock. Doesn't react with acid.

4. Contains large black flat crystals which are lined up. Some pale crystals. Very hard.

5. Dark grey/black rock all over. Doesn't react with acid.

e Look at the information Lisa's group brought back. Think about what you know about the different properties of rocks. In your group, write down the questions you would need to answer in order to identify the five rocks.

f Look again at the type of questions you need to ask. Are they similar to the useful ones you identified earlier?

Types of question

You may have found that the most useful questions are the ones that you answer with either 'yes' or 'no'. Scientists use these kinds of questions to make keys. We use keys to identify things and classify them, such as rocks, elements, plants and animals. These questions are called **closed questions** because the type of answer you can give is closed down to 'yes' or 'no'.

In contrast, an **open question** can have several possible answers. For example, 'What is the appearance of the rock?' is an open question.

g Look at these questions. In your group, decide if each one is an open or a closed question.

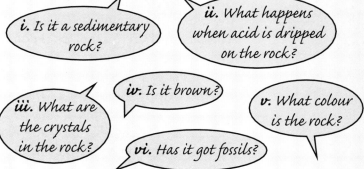

i. Is it a sedimentary rock?

ii. What happens when acid is dripped on the rock?

iii. What are the crystals in the rock?

iv. Is it brown?

v. What colour is the rock?

vi. Has it got fossils?

Questions

1. Write a key to classify the three main types of rock. Use some of the questions you have written and what you know about the properties of the three main types of rock.

2. Discuss what kind of questions is best for classifying things. Explain your answer.

3. Imagine you are going into the field to make observations and collect information about rocks. Describe how you would organise your records to make sure you come back with all the information you need to identify the rocks. Explain why you would organise your records in the way you suggest.

No relief road!

Eco-warriors

Bailiffs swooped to evict eco-warriors from the protest camp on the route of the Northern Relief Road today.

Police blocked off the entrance to the A38 at Bassetts Pole roundabout as the bailiffs approached the camp near Weeford.

A 40-strong cordon of security guards stretched across the entrance to the cottages where the protesters have created a network of underground tunnels in a bid to delay the controversial toll road.

'The role of the police at the site is to ensure the safety of the public.'

Why have a road?

The Northern Relief Road is a 27-mile long road which will take some of the traffic from the M6 motorway through Birmingham. Birmingham is the second largest city in England so the city itself is already busy. The M6 is a main route from the south of England to the north, and regularly has big traffic jams. It also has a lot of accidents because it is so busy.

The relief road will destroy large areas of countryside. This will affect many of the plants and animals that live there. The place where a plant or an animal lives is called its **habitat**. The surroundings in a habitat are called the **environment**. A habitat provides all the things plants and animals need to carry out the life processes, and also gives them shelter. The road will remove lots of different habitats.

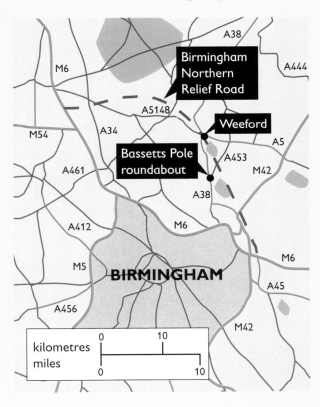

Different habitats

A habitat might be on land or in water. Examples of land habitats include fields, forests, soil and deserts. Water habitats include ponds, rivers or lakes and even salty water like the sea.

A habitat can be:
- damp or dry
- hot or cold
- light or dark.

(a) One habitat can be home to several different animals and plants. Below is a list of animals and plants that were threatened by the new road. In which habitat does each one live?

**field mice   frogs   squirrels
water beetles   birch trees   grass**

Plants and animals have adaptations that help them to survive in their habitat, so we find different plants and animals in different habitats.

b Explain why a frog and a woodpecker could not swap habitats.

Under the ground is a perfect habitat for earthworms. Worms have a pointed head to tunnel their way through the soil. It is dark under the soil, so an earthworm does not need to be able to see, but it can sense vibrations and can tell when a bird is walking on the ground above it. Earthworms feed on dead leaves which they pull under the ground.

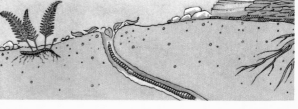

c What is the earthworm's best sense?

Ecosystem

One area like a forest or pond, including all the living things in it and also its soil, air and climate, is called an **ecosystem**.

The ecosystem of a wood has lots of shade, especially in spring and summer. Fungi like mushrooms grow in the damp soil. The air is often cool and moist. There are few grasses and flowers under the trees, but there are a lot of nuts and berries in autumn. Trees provide good nesting sites for birds and homes for climbing animals.

d This photo shows a very different ecosystem – a city. Describe what this ecosystem is like. Think about:
- the air ● the temperature
- the food available for animals
- the space for animals to live.

Decision time ...

Peter wants to help protect the ecosystems threatened by the road. He is thinking about joining the protest camp.

e What do you think about the road? Work with a partner and write down points for and against joining the protest camp.

Questions

1. What did the eco-warriors do to delay the building of the road?

2. Explain how road-building can affect both the ecosystem and different habitats.

3. An oak tree is about to be cut down in the school grounds to extend the bike sheds. How would you feel about this? What would you do?

4. This notice was in the library:

a How do volunteers with the Wildlife Trust protect the environment?
b If the relief road is built, how effective do you think replanting will be?

Plants in their habitats

There is a huge variety of plants on the Earth, and we are discovering more all the time. A group of plants of the same type is called a species. There are many unknown species, particularly in the depths of the rainforests where they are difficult to find and study.

Plants make up a large part of the environment. They provide food and shelter for animals. Scientists classify the millions of plant species into groups to make them easier to study. There are four main groups of land plants:

● flowering plants ● mosses ● ferns ● conifers.

Learn about

➤ Plant groups

Flowering plants

Grasses are flowering plants.

The biggest group of plants is the **flowering plants**. There are about 30 000 species of flowering plant on the Earth, including grasses and many trees. There is a huge variety of different leaf shapes. The flowers also vary in size and shape. Some are large and brightly coloured, while others are small and dull and difficult to spot.

Why do scientists classify such a wide range of species into one group? They do this because the group tells us something important about how the plants **reproduce**. Flowering plants reproduce using **seeds**. Seeds contain food for the new plant, and they can survive in dry or difficult conditions before they grow into a new plant.

Seeds are formed after fertilisation, when the pollen joins with the ovule. Some flowers **disperse** (spread) their pollen on the wind. Other plants have flowers with coloured and often scented petals to attract insects, and the insects then carry the pollen on their bodies to other flowers.

Flowering plants have a good water transport system. They have a waterproof waxy layer called a **cuticle** on their leaves. The cuticle stops the leaves from losing too much water, so that flowering plants can grow in a wide variety of habitats. They can grow in dry places where many other plants would fail.

The other groups of plants have different ways of reproducing. They have different kinds of leaves, stems and roots. This affects how well they can survive in different habitats.

Silver birch trees are flowering plants.

a Describe how the flowering plants are adapted to survive in a wide variety of habitats.

Mosses

Mosses do not make seeds. They reproduce by making small light **spores**, which grow into a new moss when they land in a damp place. A moss needs damp conditions for fertilisation to produce the spores.

Mosses are small plants that look like a springy cushion. They have very small, simple leaves, stems and small roots. They do not have **veins** to carry water as other plants do. Mosses dry up easily, so they have to live in wet places. Mosses grow well in boggy habitats where the soil is peat – it is wet and acidic with a layer of partly rotted dead plants.

Ferns

Ferns do not make seeds. Like mosses, they reproduce by making **spores**, and they need moisture for this. Ferns have tough leaves called **fronds**. The fronds are large and can trap sunlight well, but they dry out quite easily. Ferns also have strong roots. They grow well in damp, cool, shaded woodland habitats. Ferns are one of the oldest types of plant on Earth. They were around before the dinosaurs, and we often find fossilised ferns.

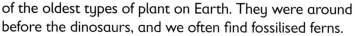

Conifers

Conifers are trees that produce seeds inside **cones**. Their pollen moves on the wind. They have a large trunk and roots. Their thin needle-like leaves have a small surface area and a cuticle, which prevents them from losing too much water. Conifers can live in very cold, frozen climates.

b Which of the four main types of plant would you expect to find in:
  i a wet peat bog?
  ii a shaded area of the garden?
  iii the slopes of a snow-covered mountain?
  iv a sunny meadow?

Questions

1. Why would you be more likely to find mosses growing under an oak tree near a duck pond than in the middle of a field?

2. **a** Describe how ferns and mosses reproduce.
   b Explain how the reproduction of ferns and mosses is different from the reproduction of flowering plants and conifers.

3. The pollen from conifers always travels on the wind. How does this make conifers different from flowering plants?

4. Conifers produce large amounts of pollen. Why do you think this is?

5. Which type of forest would you expect to find in the Arctic? Give a reason for your choice.

6. Write a key to help scientists put new plants they discover into one of the four main groups.

For your notes

Plants are classified into four groups by looking at their leaves and how they **reproduce**.

- **Flowering plants** reproduce from **seeds** and have various shapes of leaves with a waterproof **cuticle**.

- **Mosses** reproduce from **spores** and have very small leaves.

- **Ferns** reproduce from **spores** and have leaves called **fronds**.

- **Conifers** reproduce from **seeds** in **cones** and have thin, needle-like leaves.

Plants go for energy

Energetic forests

Like animals, plants need energy to carry out their life processes. Plants make their own food by photosynthesis, which happens in chloroplasts in the leaves. Plants need carbon dioxide and water for photosynthesis. They take in carbon dioxide through their leaves and water through their roots. Chlorophyll absorbs the light energy needed for the reaction.

carbon dioxide + water → glucose + oxygen   **light energy taken in**

In the daytime, when it is light, plants take in carbon dioxide from the air and use light energy from the Sun for photosynthesis. Photosynthesis produces **glucose**, and also oxygen as a waste product. Photosynthesis transfers light energy to chemical energy. At night, when it is dark, photosynthesis does not happen.

Respiration

Plants and animals break down their food to release the chemical energy from it. This process is called **respiration** and it happens in all plant cells just as it does in animal cells. Glucose and oxygen react, producing carbon dioxide and water, and releasing energy. We call this **aerobic respiration** because it uses oxygen from the air. In plants, the glucose comes from photosynthesis.

ⓐ Write a word equation for respiration.

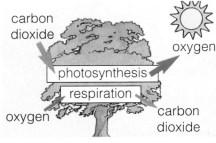

Photosynthesis is faster than respiration.

The whole picture

Respiration happens all the time, day and night. In the daytime, a plant gets its oxygen for respiration from photosynthesis.

During the day, photosynthesis is faster than respiration, so plants give out the oxygen they don't need into the air. At night photosynthesis stops, so plants take oxygen out of the air for respiration. It is important to keep the right balance of oxygen and carbon dioxide in the air.

ⓑ Why is photosynthesis important to animals?

Root cells need oxygen from the air for respiration too. If the soil is waterlogged, all of the air spaces in the soil are filled with water. The roots cannot get enough oxygen and the plant will die.

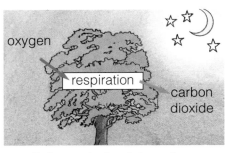

Only respiration takes place.

Balancing act

A group of scientists used sensors to measure carbon dioxide levels in a greenhouse between dawn and dusk. Look at the graph.

(c) At what times was the amount of carbon dioxide produced by respiration equal to the amount of carbon dioxide used by photosynthesis? Explain how you worked out your answer.

(d) When was most carbon dioxide absorbed from the air?

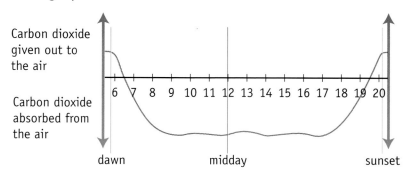

Carbon dioxide given out to the air

Carbon dioxide absorbed from the air

6 7 8 9 10 11 12 13 14 15 16 17 18 19 20

dawn   midday   sunset

For my next experiment ...

Professor Chloe Dupont was trying to convince her students that both plants and animals respire. She set up a respiration chamber to show them that plants produce carbon dioxide by respiration. The respiration chamber apparatus is shown in the diagram.

The professor placed a green plant on the bench under a bell jar, and put a black cloth around the outside to stop the plant from photosynthesising. The limewater turned milky.

(e) Why did photosynthesis stop?

(f) How do we know that the plant was respiring?

She took away the black cloth, used fresh limewater and replaced the plant with a mouse.

(g) What do you think happened?

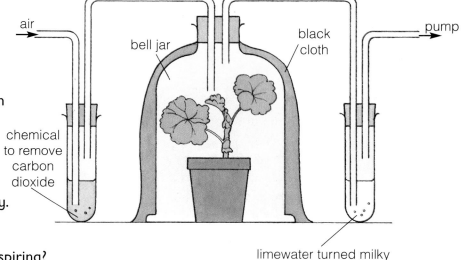

air

bell jar

black cloth

pump

chemical to remove carbon dioxide

limewater turned milky

Questions

1. a List: i the reactants ii the products for photosynthesis.
   b List: i the reactants ii the products for respiration.
   c Give two reasons why animals could not live without plants.
   d Could plants live without animals?

2. Which gas do plants make during the day and at night?

3. Plants are often taken out of hospital wards at night. Can you think of a reason for this? (Include the word equation for respiration in your answer.)

4. Chopping down rainforests gives us more land to graze cattle, so we can have cheaper burgers. What are the disadvantages of this?

For your notes

Plants release energy from food by **respiration**, in the same way as animals do.

Respiration takes place in every cell of a plant.

Growing and growing

Green fingers

Plants need **carbon**, **hydrogen** and **oxygen** for growth. These elements are all present in the glucose that plants make by photosynthesis. The plant uses some of the glucose it makes for respiration. It converts the rest of the glucose to substances it needs for growth:
- cellulose for cell walls
- starch which stores energy
- fats and oils in seeds
- sugars in fruits.

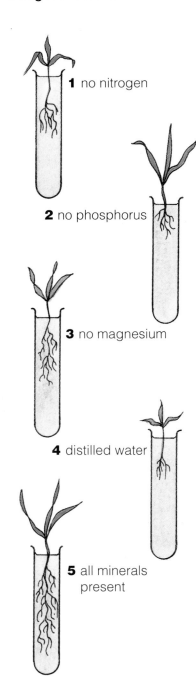

1 no nitrogen

2 no phosphorus

3 no magnesium

4 distilled water

5 all minerals present

Learn about

▶ Plant growth

▶ Biomass

Did you know?

Plants don't need soil to grow! Hydroponics is growing plants in solutions instead of soil. The solutions contain all the mineral salts the plant needs to grow.

The plant also makes other substances for growth, such as proteins to make new cells. To make some of these substances from glucose, the plant needs other elements as well as carbon, hydrogen and oxygen. For example, it needs **nitrogen**, **phosphorus** and **magnesium**. The plant takes these elements in through its roots from the soil. These elements are present in salts called **mineral salts** that are dissolved in water in the soil. Nitrogen is used to make proteins for healthy growth. Phosphorus is needed for strong roots, and magnesium is needed to make chlorophyll. Farmers add fertilisers to the soil to give the crops extra mineral salts to improve their growth.

Heather and Julie set up an experiment. They grew barley seedlings in water containing different mineral salts. The diagram on the left shows this.

(a) Copy and complete the table to show their results.

(b) Explain why the seedling in tube 4 did not grow very well.

Seedling	Observations
1	
2	
3	
4	
5	

Feeling hungry

A caterpillar is a **herbivore**, which means it feeds on plants. A caterpillar eats a massive amount of plant food, which it uses to store energy in its body. When it reaches a certain size, it spins a **cocoon** around itself. It stays inside the cocoon for more than two weeks. The caterpillar does not eat while it is in the cocoon. It uses its stored energy to rearrange its body. Eventually, the caterpillar breaks through the cocoon as a butterfly.

(c) Why does a caterpillar need to eat so much food?

Passing on biomass

The mass of all the material in a living thing, not including the water, is called its **biomass**. In a plant, photosynthesis produces the biomass of the plant. When a caterpillar eats a leaf, some of the plant biomass in the leaf becomes part of the caterpillar. However, not all the plant biomass eaten by the caterpillar becomes caterpillar biomass. Otherwise, a caterpillar that ate 1 kg of cabbage leaves would weigh more than 1 kg. Can you imagine a caterpillar that weighs 1 kg?

Around 10% of the plant biomass eaten by a caterpillar becomes caterpillar biomass.

d Roughly how many grams of biomass would be transferred to a caterpillar that ate 100 g of cabbage leaves?

Where does the rest go?

Some of the food eaten by an animal such as a caterpillar ends up as biomass in the animal. The rest of the food eaten does not become animal biomass. Some of it is used by the animal in respiration to release energy. This energy is used for the life processes such movement, reproduction, excretion and keeping warm. The rest of the food is excreted as waste.

Plants make glucose by photosynthesis. They use some of the glucose to make plant biomass. They use the rest for respiration.

Some of the food is used for respiration. This produces energy to move, reproduce, excrete and keep warm.

Some of the food is used for growth and becomes part of the caterpillar's body (biomass).

Some of the energy from respiration is wasted as heat energy lost to the surroundings.

Some of the food is not digested and passes out as waste.

Questions

1. **a** Which elements does a plant need to make cellulose?
   b Where in the plants is the cellulose found?

2. Why is a caterpillar described as a herbivore?

3. Explain the meaning of the word 'biomass'.

4. A rabbit eats 1 kg of carrots. Use the caterpillar example to estimate its increase in biomass and explain why it does not become 1 kg heavier after its meal.

5. The rabbit takes in 100 units of energy from the carrots. It uses 40 units for respiration. 50 units are excreted in waste and lost as heat energy to the surroundings.
   a How many units of energy from the carrots does the rabbit convert to biomass?
   b What percentage of the energy from the carrots is lost to the surroundings?
   c Where does the remaining energy from the carrots go?

For your notes

As well as **carbon, oxygen** and **hydrogen**, plants need **nitrogen** and other elements for growth.

The total mass of a living thing, not including the water, is called its **biomass**.

Some of the energy from the biomass eaten by an animal is used for growth and converted to animal biomass. The rest is used for the life processes or lost to the environment.

Environment

8.5

Home alone?

Woodland food chains

If you are walking through a wood in the spring or summer and look closely at the leaves, you might see a caterpillar feeding on a leaf. If you are patient, you might see the second link in the food chain – a bird swooping down to eat the caterpillar.

A **food chain** shows the links between the organisms in an ecosystem. It shows which animals feed on other animals or on plants. The arrows show what eats what, and the direction of the energy transfer. Most food chains start with a plant. The plant makes its own food by photosynthesis using light energy from the Sun, carbon dioxide and water.

The green plants produce the food, so they are called **producers**. The animals consume (eat) the plants or other animals, so they are called **consumers**. Animals that eat plants, such as rabbits and field mice, are called **herbivores**. Larger animals such as foxes and owls, that eat other animals, are called **carnivores**. Energy is transferred through the food chain when one organism eats another.

Learn about

➤ Food webs

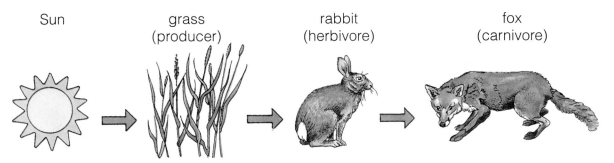

Sun   grass   rabbit   fox
        (producer) (herbivore) (carnivore)

(a) Look at the food chain in the diagram. Which word would describe both the herbivore and the carnivore?

Pyramids of numbers

A rabbit eats lots of grass plants. Several rabbits will feed just one fox. If you look at the number of producers, herbivores and carnivores in this food chain, you can build a pyramid. There are fewer and fewer consumers as you go up this food chain. This is because energy is lost from the food chain to the environment at each feeding stage. Energy is lost because all the biomass eaten by a consumer does not get converted to new biomass in the consumer – some of it is used for respiration or excreted.

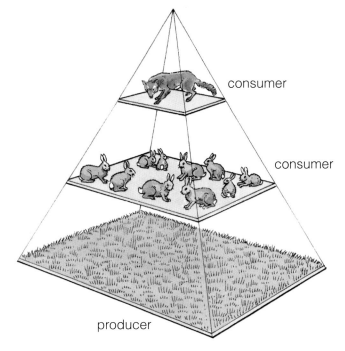

consumer

consumer

producer

114

Predators

Animals that hunt other animals for food are called **predators**. The animals they eat are called their **prey**. Foxes are predators because they hunt rabbits and eat them. The rabbits are their prey. In the 1950s a disease called myxomatosis killed many of the rabbits in the countryside.

b Describe two effects of this disease on the food chain.

c Why do you think that more foxes were seen in towns after that time?

Food webs

Rabbits are not the only animals that eat grass. Lots of food chains in a wood link together to make a **food web**. In a food web, there are several food chains with species in common. In the food web below, both rabbits and field mice eat grass.

d How many food chains can you find in this food web?

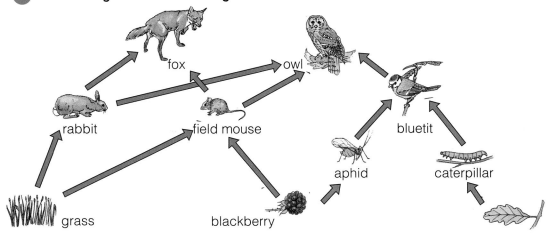

Dead bodies

Bacteria and fungi in the soil are also part of the food web. They are called **decomposers** because they feed on dead bodies. They break them down, returning useful elements such as nitrogen, magnesium and phosphorus to the soil.

Questions

1. Draw a food chain with three links, including humans as one of the links.

2. Make a food web by adding one producer and one herbivore to your food chain.

3. Explain why food chains start with a green plant.

4. What do the arrows in a food web show?

5. A large number of deer once lived on the Kaibab plateau north of the Grand Canyon in Arizona, USA. In 1907 their predators, wolves, coyotes and pumas, were killed to protect the deer. What do you think happened?

6. Decomposers are not always shown on a food web. What do they do? Why are they important?

For your notes

A **food chain** shows which organisms eat which others in an ecosystem. A food chain shows the direction of energy transfer.

Food chains are linked to make **food webs**.

Green plants are **producers**. Animals are **consumers**.

Predators are animals that hunt other animals for food. These are their **prey**.

Decomposers feed on dead bodies in the food web.

Food for thought

Tempting treat?

Wendy's mum decided not to buy Gran's favourite Belgian chocolates for her birthday.

Mum explained, 'The scientists have found some poisonous substances called dioxins in the prepared food that they feed the farm animals in Belgium. The dioxins must have come from factory waste that has got into the food. The chickens have been poisoned. We have been warned that any meat, butter, milk and eggs could be contaminated. The chocolates might have been made from contaminated milk. Some of them might have eggs in them.'

(a) How could Belgian chocolates have become contaminated?

There has been a government health warning.

Dioxins

Dioxins are waste products of industrial processes. They are made in paper factories as part of the bleaching process. They are also made when rubbish is burned, and they are found in diesel exhaust fumes. Low doses of dioxins are safe, but large doses can cause cancer, other serious illnesses and even death. Waste that contains dioxins or other poisonous substances is called **toxic waste**.

TOXIC

The Belgian dioxin disaster was discovered when eggs were not hatching and chicks were ill. The problem was traced back to their food, which could also have been eaten by pigs or cattle.

Toxic build-up

Some poisonous substances like dioxins are not used up by the animal's body. They are not excreted either – they are stored in the body. When this animal is eaten by another animal, the substance is passed on through the food chain.

If the dioxin molecules are spread out, the **concentration** is low. If there are more dioxin particles in the same volume, the particles will be closer together and the concentration is higher.

low concentration in chicken food

high concentration in person

Chickens eat a large amount of food during their lives. There may only be a low concentration of dioxin in the food, but the chickens keep all the dioxin they eat in their bodies. The dioxin builds up in the chickens. The dioxin becomes more concentrated as you go up the food chain. The amount of dioxin that a person gets depends on how many chickens or eggs they eat.

b Why is it difficult to say how great the health risk is to humans?

Metals

Some metals such as lead and mercury are toxic and can be passed through food chains. Minemata Bay is on the coast of Japan. In the 1950s, many people were killed or disabled as a result of mercury poisoning. The mercury was in the waste from a plastics factory that flowed into the sea. It got into the fish and the people were poisoned when they ate the fish.

c The people at Minemata ate a lot of fish. Explain how the concentration of mercury could be higher in a person than in a fish.

Lead causes brain damage and eventually death. Children who are exposed to high levels of lead do less well at school and have behaviour problems. Lead used to be added to petrol to make engines run more smoothly. Lead pollution came out of car exhausts, finding its way into the soil and plants and contaminating food chains. Leaded petrol has now been banned and other chemicals are added to petrol instead.

d What evidence is there that we might be exposed to lead naturally through the food chain as well as through industrial activity?

> **Did you know?**
>
> Eight litres of contaminated oil is enough to produce 1600 tonnes of feed, and this is enough to feed 16 million chickens for one day.

> **Did you know?**
>
> The bones of a Stone Age woman and three children have been found in Dorset. The lead levels in their teeth were almost as high as the lead levels in our teeth today. Scientists think that Stone Age people might have eaten food contaminated with lead that has come from rocks into the soil. We might have underestimated how much lead we are getting in this way.

It's just a scare, there are dioxins in the air and in our food anyway.

Dioxins stay in your body.

I don't want to get cancer.

Low doses of dioxins are safe.

Questions

1. There was a phone-in on the radio about the Belgian chocolates. Some of the comments are shown on the right.

   What do you think? Should Wendy have bought the Belgian chocolates? Write an argument to support your point of view.

2. What happens to the concentration of dioxin as it goes up the food chain?

3. Some of the chemicals that were used to kill insects on crops have been banned because the numbers of birds like the owl and hawk were being affected. Why do you think the birds were dying?

4. What can be done to prevent toxic industrial waste from poisoning the food chain?

> **For your notes**
>
> Toxic substances can be passed on and build up in food chains.

special daisies

Not many left?

Students Joan and Lydia think they have found a rare variety of daisy growing among the ordinary daisies in a field that is to be dug up. The daisy has a bright pink tinge to its petals and grows well in moist conditions. Look at the map of the field.

On the map, 1 mm represents 1 m of the field. There are 1000 mm in a metre, so 1 mm on the map means 1000 mm in the field. We call this a **ratio** of 1:1000. Any measurements on the map need to be multiplied by 1000 to give the real distance in the field.

Think about
- Ratios
- Sampling

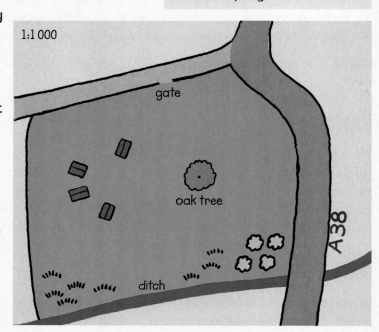

1:1 000

gate

oak tree

A38

ditch

(a) Measure the distance from the gate to the middle of the largest oak tree on the map.

(b) Work out the real distance in metres from the gate to the oak tree.

The Northfield Conservation Group wants to find out how many of the daisy plants are in the field. The evidence from their work might save the area from the developers.

Sampling

Joan thought they could count all the rare daisy plants in the field. Lydia suggested that instead of this they should look at a few small areas of the field as samples. 'We could find an area with lots of the daisies, and do our samples there,' she said. 'But that wouldn't be fair,' said Joan. 'It won't tell us the total number in the field.'

They decided that the fairest way of finding out how many of the daisies there are in the field without counting them all was to do **random samples**. This means doing samples in different places without choosing the places deliberately.

(c) Why do you think they decided not to count every single rare daisy plant in the field?

Joan and Lydia used a **quadrat** to do their sampling. A quadrat is a wooden frame measuring 1 m on all four sides. This means it has an area of 1 m^2 (one square metre).

Joan threw a quadrat over her shoulder without looking where it would land. Then she looked at the ground inside the quadrat and counted the number of the daisy plants inside. She threw the quadrat and counted the daisy plants 10 times.

(d) How did Joan make sure her quadrats were placed randomly?

(e) How big an area of field did Joan study? (How big was her sample?)

Joan's results

Throw number	Number of rare daisy plants
1	0
2	0
3	0
4	3
5	0
6	0
7	0
8	0
9	0
10	6

Joan and Lydia found 9 rare daisy plants in Joan's sample.

The whole sample had an area of 10 m². The field covers 4000 m² in total. So the **ratio** of the area they sampled to the whole field is 1:400.

The ratio of the number of plants in the sample to the number of plants in the field is the same, 1:400. So to find the number of plants in the whole field, they multiplied the number in the sample by 400.

f How many plants did they think might be in the field?

g Will this be the exact number of plants in the field?

A bigger sample

Lydia was still worried that most of the quadrats might have landed in parts of the field where there were not many of the daisy plants. This would mean their number for the total rare daisy plants in the field would be lower than the real number. She insisted that they do some more throws to get a more accurate result. So they did 20 new throws, 10 each. Here are the results:

Lydia		Joan	
Throw number	Number of rare daisy plants	Throw number	Number of rare daisy plants
1	0	1	0
2	0	2	3
3	3	3	0
4	0	4	0
5	0	5	0
6	0	6	0
7	0	7	4
8	5	8	0
9	1	9	0
10	0	10	0

h How many rare daisy plants did Joan and Lydia find in these 20 new throws?

i What is the ratio of the area of the new sample to the area of the whole field?

j How many plants might there be in the whole field based on the new sample?

Questions

1. a How accurate do you think Joan and Lydia's experiments were?

   b How could they have made the experiments more reliable? Think about where the daisy prefers to grow.

2. Do you think the special daisy plants are rare? What other information would you need to help you decide?

The concert

There is going to be a concert to raise money for charity. Lots of local orchestras, choirs and bands are going to play at the concert, which will be followed by a fireworks display. Amigo's father is on the committee organising the concert. He is responsible for arranging the venue and the rehearsals.

Rehearsals

The concert and firework display is in the evening. Amigo goes with his father in the afternoon, to watch everything being set up. The concert is in a big field. There are two main stages: one for the orchestras and choirs and one for the bands. Amigo watches an orchestra rehearsing. The musicians are tuning their instruments.

a What part of these instruments vibrates to make sound?

> violin   drum   trumpet   xylophone   oboe

Amigo goes over to the other stage. A band is rehearsing. The band has a lead singer, a drummer, a keyboard player and two guitarists. The band uses electric instruments, microphones, amplifiers and loudspeakers.

b Which device takes in sound energy and gives out electrical energy?

c Which device takes in electrical energy and gives out sound energy?

Amigo sits on the edge of the stage. He is so close that he can see the large cone of the loudspeaker moving in and out. There is a lot of bass in the music. Even with his fingers in his ears he can feel the music.

d Explain how the moving cone produces sounds that people can hear.

e Why can Amigo 'feel' the music?

The performance

It was soon time for the concert to begin. Amigo was sitting with Gareth, a sound engineer from the local radio station. The concert was being broadcast live. Gareth explained that it was difficult to broadcast a concert with so many different acts because of the variation in the sound they made.

f Describe how the sounds made by the acts could vary.

g Gareth measured the amplitude and the frequency of the sounds. What does:
  i the amplitude
  ii the frequency
  of the sound tell Gareth?

Amigo enjoyed the concert, but he was looking forward most to the firework display. He was not disappointed. There were many spectacular rockets. One rocket was huge. It exploded high up in the air. Amigo saw the colours of the explosion first, both up in the sky and mirrored in the lake. Then he heard the sound the rocket had made when it exploded. Then he heard the sound again. The second sound was quieter than the first.

Questions

1. a Draw a diagram showing how Amigo sees:
  i the rocket exploding in the air
  ii the image of the explosion in the water.
  b Explain why Amigo saw the explosion before he heard it.
  c What was the fainter sound that Amigo heard later?

2. Draw an energy transfer diagram for a firework exploding.

3. Amigo saw the explosion before he heard it. Think of two other situations where you see something before you hear it.

4. The fireworks were reflected in the lake. Explain why Amigo saw an image when he looked at the lake, but not when he looked at the grass.

5. Compare an electric guitar with an ordinary guitar:
  a What vibrates to produce each note?
  b How is the sound made loud enough for people to hear?

Learn about

► How light travels

► How we see light

Sources and shadows

Sunlight comes from the Sun. Candlelight comes from the flame of a candle. Electric light comes from a filament lamp. Light comes from a **source**. The source gives out light energy, which travels away from the source in all directions.

(a) Make a list of 10 different sources of light.

Light travels from the source in straight lines. If the light is blocked, a **shadow** is formed.

(b) Look at the shadow on the cinema screen. How could the shadow be made:
   i bigger?   **ii** smaller?

Cameras

The simplest type of camera is a tiny hole in a piece of card. It works best with a hole made with a pin, so it is called a pinhole camera. You can use a pinhole camera to make a picture on a screen, or a permanent image on film. Pinhole cameras work because light travels in straight lines.

Look at the diagram of the pinhole camera and the flame. Light from the tip of the flame travels outwards in all directions. Some of the light from the tip of the flame goes through the pinhole. This is shown by an arrow. Light from the base of the flame also travels out in all directions. Again, some of the light goes through the pinhole. This is shown by the other arrow. Where these arrows hit the screen you see a picture or **image**. As you can see, the image is upside down, or **inverted**.

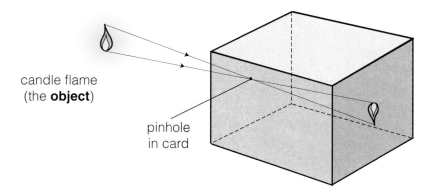

candle flame
(the **object**)

pinhole
in card

picture on
screen
(the **image**)

(c) Look at the diagram of the pinhole camera. Imagine that the same camera was moved closer to the flame. Is the image of the flame bigger or smaller?

(d) Look at the diagram of the pinhole camera. Imagine using a longer pinhole camera with the pinhole the same distance from the flame. Is the image of the flame bigger or smaller?

More complicated cameras

Cameras are now much more sophisticated than a simple pinhole camera. The hole in a camera is called the **aperture**, and the size of the aperture can be changed to let in more or less light. The film inside the camera is protected by the **shutter**, which only opens when the picture is being taken. Modern cameras also contain a **lens**. The lens makes sure that the image is always sharp, no matter how far the photographer is from the object, or how big the aperture is. We say that a sharp image is **focused** or **in focus**.

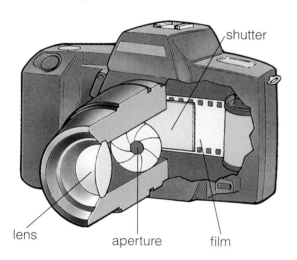

lens   aperture   film

Eyes

Eyes are similar to pinhole cameras. Light enters the eye and forms an inverted image on the back of the eye. Some animals have very simple eyes, no more complicated than a pinhole camera. Look at the diagram of a very simple animal eye. The eye is like a cave with a very small entrance. The small hole allows light into the eye. The eye is lined with light-sensitive cells at the back (shown in yellow). An inverted image forms on these light-sensitive cells.

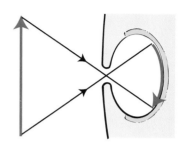

Our eyes are more complicated, like a modern camera. The aperture in our eye is the **pupil**, and the size of the pupil can be changed to let in more or less light. Each eye has a shutter, the eyelid, and a lens to make sure the image is always focused.

Special cells in the back of the eye take in the light energy

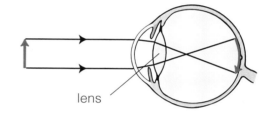

lens

and give out electrical energy, which is sent along nerves to the brain. The image on the back of the eye is inverted, just like the image made by the pinhole camera. Your brain turns the image the right way up.

Questions

1. Look at the diagram of the pinhole camera. Imagine a pinhole camera with two pinholes. Draw a ray diagram showing the image on the screen and how the image is formed.

2. Write a definition for each of these words:

    image   object   inverted   shadow   light source

3. Study the diagrams of the camera and the human eye on this page.
    a In what ways are the camera and the eye the same?
    b In what ways are the camera and the eye different?
    c Draw a ray diagram of a camera, like the diagram of the eye. Use a red arrow as the object, and show the image with another red arrow. Draw the film in yellow. Show the lens, the aperture and the shutter. Use a ruler to draw straight lines to show the light travelling. Add arrows.

For your notes

Light travels away from its source in all directions.

Light travels in straight lines.

We see because light enters our eyes.

A thought experiment

Imagine you are in a black room. The walls are black, the floor is black, the ceiling is black and the door is black. There are no windows. Every part of your body is covered in black clothes. Your face is covered in a black mask with holes for you to see through. There is a lamp hanging from the ceiling. It has a black light fitting. You switch it on using a black switch.

You would see a bright light bulb. You would see nothing else. You see the light bulb because some of the light from the light bulb is entering your eye. The rest of the light is soaked up when it hits the black surfaces. We say the light is **absorbed**.

You take a tennis ball from your pocket. You would now see the ball. The ball is not black. Not all of the light hitting the ball is absorbed. Some of the light is **reflected**. Some of the light from the lamp hits the ball, bounces off and enters your eyes.

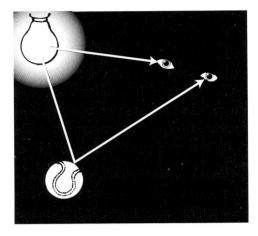

a Explain what the words 'absorbed' and 'reflected' mean when used about light.

The law of reflection

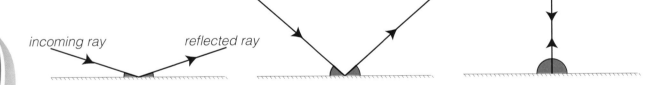

incoming ray   *reflected ray*

When light reflects off a surface, we can predict where it will go. We can use a thin beam of light, a **ray**, to investigate reflection.

Look at the diagrams. They show what happens when a ray of light bounces off a flat surface such as a mirror. The arrows show the direction the light is going. As you can see, the angle between the incoming ray and the mirror is equal to the angle between the reflected ray and the mirror.

Scientists did not use this angle when they made up their law of reflection. This is because not all surfaces are flat. Some are curved, and some are uneven. It is difficult to measure the angle between the rays and a curved or uneven surface. Instead scientists use the angle between the ray and a line called the **normal**.

Look at the diagram near the top of the page opposite. The normal is a line at 90° to the surface if the surface is flat. If the surface is not flat, you have to find the normal by doing an experiment. If a ray hits the surface and is reflected back the way it came, it was travelling along the normal. This is shown in the diagram to the left. Look at the other two diagrams. The angle between the incoming ray and the normal is equal to the angle between the reflected ray and the normal.

b What is a ray?

c How do you find the normal?

We call the angle between the incoming ray and the normal the **angle of incidence**, labelled *i* in the diagrams. We call the angle between the reflected ray and the normal the **angle of reflection**, labelled *r* in the diagrams.

The law of reflection

The angle of incidence equals the angle of reflection.

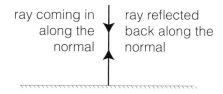

ray coming in along the normal | ray reflected back along the normal

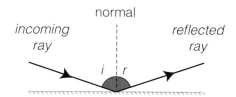

incoming ray | normal | reflected ray

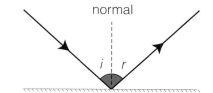

normal

Scattering

Most surfaces are not perfectly flat and smooth. Even the paper this book is made of has many tiny bumps on its surface. When light hits the paper, it is **scattered** in all directions. Look at the diagram of rays of light hitting paper. The light rays come in from the same direction, but are scattered in many different directions.

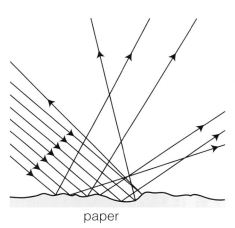

paper

Mirrors

A mirror has a perfectly smooth surface. Look at the diagram of rays of light hitting a mirror. The light rays come in from the same direction and the rays are all reflected in the same direction. This is why you can see an image of your face when you look in a mirror, but not when you look at a piece of paper.

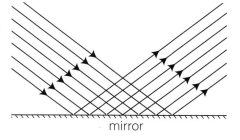

mirror

d Explain why a dirty knife will not act as a mirror, but a clean knife will.

Questions

1. Imagine yourself in a black room like the one described in the thought experiment. You are wearing black clothes and gloves. You take out a box of matches and strike a match. What would you see? Explain why you would see these things and not others. Use the words 'reflect' and 'absorb' in your answer.

2. What is the law of reflection?

3. A periscope is an instrument used to look over a wall, or to look above the surface of the water when you are under the water. Design a periscope using two mirrors. Be careful to explain exactly how the mirrors should be placed. Draw a diagram showing how your periscope works.

4. A puddle can act as a mirror.
   a Explain why, using a diagram.
   b The image is broken up when a pebble drops into the puddle. Why is the image broken up?

For your notes

When light hits a surface, it is **absorbed** or **reflected**.

The **angle of incidence** equals the **angle of reflection**.

Most surfaces **scatter** light.

Mirrors do not scatter the light because they are smooth.

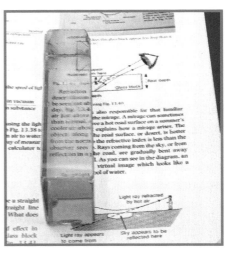

Transparent materials

Light can travel through some materials. These materials are **transparent**, or see-through. If a material lets no light through, we say it is **opaque**. If a material only lets some of the light through, we call it a **translucent** material.

A trick of the light

You often see strange effects when light passes through a transparent material like water or glass. Swimming pools look shallower than they really are, a pencil in a bowl of water looks bent and text looks closer and larger when looked at through a glass block.

Air to glass

These strange effects happen because the light bends when it goes from one material to another. We call this bending **refraction**. We can investigate refraction using a block of glass.

Look at the left-hand diagram. It shows what happens when a ray of light enters glass at 90°, along the normal. The light does not bend. Look at the other two diagrams. When the ray of light hits the glass at an angle, it bends. It bends towards the normal.

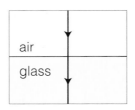

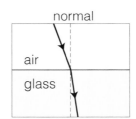

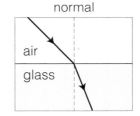

Why does it bend?

The light refracts because it travels at different speeds in different materials. Light travels faster in air than in water or glass. When the light hits the boundary at 90°, all the light slows down at the same time, so the ray stays straight. If the light hits the boundary at an angle, some of the light slows down first, making a bend. One way of thinking about this is to imagine a truck driving into mud. If the truck hits the mud straight on (along the normal), then both sides of the truck slow down at the same time and the truck goes in a straight line. If the truck hits the mud at an angle, then one wheel slows down before the other and the truck swings around.

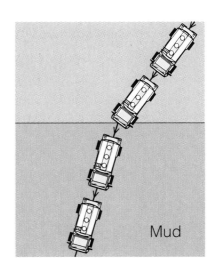

Mud

a Light refracts when it goes from air to glass at an angle. Does it bend towards the normal or away from the normal?

b Does light refract when it goes from air to glass along the normal?

Water to air

Refraction also happens when light travels from glass to air, or from water to air. Look at the diagram on the right. It shows a coin at the bottom of a beaker of water. Light is reflected from the coin. A ray of this light is shown by the arrow. As the ray passes from water to air, it bends or refracts. This time it bends away from the normal, because light travels faster in air than in water.

Your brain thinks that light travels in straight lines. You see the coin higher up, where the light appeared to come from.

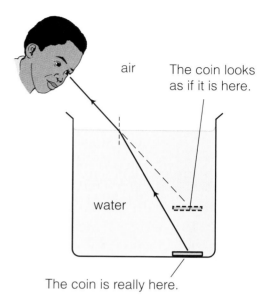

air　　The coin looks as if it is here.

water

The coin is really here.

Archer fish hunt by shooting water at insects flying above the water. The archer fish have to learn to allow for refraction.

c **i** Draw a ray diagram of an archer fish looking at an insect. Use the diagram of the coin in the beaker to help you, but remember that the light travels from the insect to the fish's eye.

　ii Will the archer fish have to shoot high or shoot low to hit the insect?

Questions

1. Refraction does not always happen when light goes from one transparent material to another. What two things must happen for refraction to take place?

2. Light travels at different speeds in air, water and perspex. It travels fastest in air, slower in water and slowest in perspex.
  a When light travels at an angle from air to water, the light slows down and refracts towards the normal. Predict what happens when light travels at an angle from:
    i water to air **ii** air to perspex **iii** water to perspex.
  b Of the experiments described above, which will make the light bend most?

For your notes

When light goes from one **transparent** material to another, it may **refract** (bend).

The light must enter the new material at an angle for refraction to happen.

Light has to travel at different speeds in the different transparent materials for this to happen.

Coloured light

Splitting white light

When you pass sunlight through a prism, the white light splits up into many colours. We call the colours produced a **spectrum**. The splitting up is called **dispersion**. White light is made up of many colours.

The colours are always in the same order: red, orange, yellow, green, blue, indigo and violet. The light has refracted twice, once when the light entered the glass and again when the light re-entered the air. The violet light bends most and the red light bends least. The difference in refraction spreads the colours.

(a) Which colour refracts the most?

(b) Which colour refracts the least?

A rainbow is made because water droplets in the air act like tiny prisms. The light is refracted as it enters and exits the water. Different colours are refracted different amounts, so the colours spread out, making a rainbow.

Learn about

➤ White light

➤ Coloured light

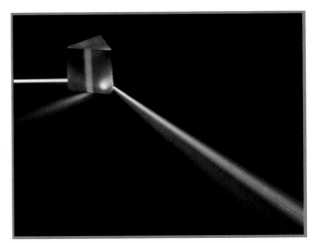

Did you know?

Many children in Britain learn the colours of the spectrum using this mnemonic:

Richard **o**f **Y**ork **g**ave **b**attle **i**n **v**ain.

Coloured filters

Look at the photo of a stained glass window. White light falls on the window, but coloured light comes through the window and enters our eyes. Some colours in the light are absorbed by the coloured glass and some colours are allowed through, or **transmitted**. The red glass transmits red light and absorbs the other colours. In the same way, the green glass transmits green light and absorbs the other colours.

white light falls on the glass

green light comes through – other colours absorbed

red light comes through – other colours absorbed

blue light comes through – other colours absorbed

(c) Look at the diagram.
What would you see if the light shone onto the window was:
i red light?   **ii** blue light?   **iii** green light?

Seeing by reflection

A red surface reflects red light. The red light enters our eyes and we see red. If we shine white light onto a red surface, the red light is reflected and the other colours are absorbed.

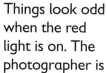

Photographers develop their film in a darkroom. They use a special red light to see what they are doing. The red light does not affect the film.

Things look odd when the red light is on. The photographer is wearing a white shirt, but it looks red. She is wearing green trousers, but they look black.

d Why does the white shirt look red?

e Why do the trousers look black?

f What happens to the red light when it hits the trousers?

Plants reject green

When we think of plants we think 'green', but plants do not use green light. Green leaves reflect green light and absorb the other colours. The reflected green light enters our eyes, so we see green leaves.

What is colour?

Different colours have different frequencies, just like different sounds have different frequencies. Colour is like pitch, and each colour is like a different musical note. The diagram below shows the frequencies of light that humans can see.

We have names for seven colours, but the spectrum contains many more than seven colours. Isaac Newton, the great scientist who made many of the discoveries about colour, chose to name seven colours because there were seven notes in a musical scale.

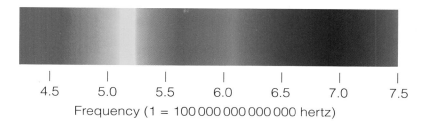

4.5	5.0	5.5	6.0	6.5	7.0	7.5

Frequency (1 = 100 000 000 000 000 hertz)

Questions

1. Conor is investigating light using coloured filters. He does the experiments shown in the diagram. What colours of light (if any) will he see at **A**, **B**, **C** and **D**?

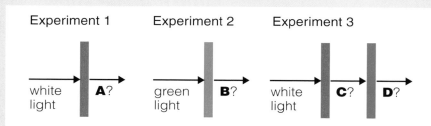

Experiment 1   Experiment 2   Experiment 3

white light   **A**?   green light   **B**?   white light   **C**?   **D**?

2. Eileen goes to a club. The club is having a 70s night with a disco. The lights flash green, blue and red. Eileen is wearing a white shirt, a red skirt and black boots.

What will Eileen's shirt, skirt and boots look like when:
a the red light is on?
b the blue light is on?
c the green light is on?

Give an explanation for each of your answers.

3. Plants need light to make food. What would happen if you tried to grow plants under green lights? Explain your answer.

For your notes

White light can be split into different colours. This is called **dispersion**.

A red, green or blue filter only allows one colour of light through and absorbs the others.

A coloured object reflects the colour we see and absorbs the other colours.

Combinations

Joe's form has been collecting copper coins for a charity. Joe is counting the money and putting it into bags. There are three possible **combinations**: only 1p coins in a bag, only 2p coins in a bag or a bag of mixed 1p and 2p coins. The coins can be combined in three different ways, to make three different combinations. You can read more about combinations in the blue box on the opposite page.

Primary colours of light

Look at the photo. It shows a television screen magnified many times. You can see that the screen is made up of dots. There are three colours of dot: red, green and blue.

Red, green and blue are the three **primary colours** of light. All colours of light can be made from combining these colours.

a How many different combinations can you make out of red, green and blue?

Secondary colours

Colours of light other than red, green and blue are made by mixing red, green and blue light. These colours are called **secondary colours**. Look at the colour chart. It shows what happens when you combine red, green and blue light. For example, colour **E** is made by combining **A** with **C**.

b Copy this table and use the colour chart to fill in the gaps.

Position	Colour	Which of red, green and blue?
A	Red	
B	Blue	
C	Green	
D	**Magenta**	
E	**Yellow**	
F	**Cyan**	
G	White	

Think about

➤ Combinations

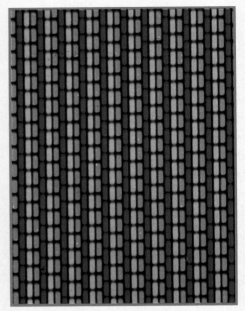

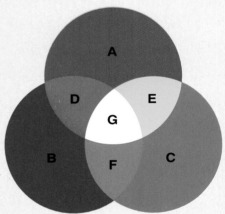

Lighting the show

Zahir wanted to help with the lighting for school productions. Miss Lawrence said that he had to learn about colour. She set him a test.

c Do the 'Lighting test' in the green box on the opposite page.

d Mark your answers (see the bottom of the next page).

Zahir scored 7/10. He could not do questions 8, 9 and 10.

e Write down what you would say to explain questions 8, 9 and 10 to Zahir. Draw any diagrams that you would use.

An example of combinations

Jane has bought some decorations in a sale. She has stars, snowflakes, angels and reindeer. How many different combinations can she make?

Jane can have each type of decoration on its own (stars; snowflakes; angels; reindeer).

Jane can have 2 types of decoration together (stars and snowflakes; stars and angels; stars and reindeer; snowflakes and angels; snowflakes and reindeer; angels and reindeer).

Jane can have 3 types of decorations together (stars, snowflakes and angels; stars, snowflakes and reindeer; stars, angels and reindeer; snowflakes, angels and reindeer).

Jane can have all 4 types of decoration together (stars, snowflakes, angels and reindeer).

So there are 15 different types of combination.

Lighting test

Imagine you only have 3 spotlights, a red, a green and a blue. What combinations of red, green and blue do you use to make the following colours?

1. Yellow.   **2.** Cyan.

3. Magenta.   **4.** White.

You can change the colour of a spotlight by putting in different filters. What combination of <u>primary</u> colours gets through each filter?

5. Red filter.   **6.** Yellow filter.

7. Cyan filter.

You can put more than one filter in a white spotlight. What colour of light would you get with these combinations of filters?

8. Yellow and cyan.   **9.** Magenta and cyan.

10. Magenta and yellow.

Seeing colours

We see colour because we have light receptors called **cones** in the backs of our eyes. We see three primary colours because we have three types of cone. One type is sensitive to red light, one to green light and one to blue light. People who are colour-blind have a fault in one or more of these types of cone.

Some fish have four types of cone.

f How many primary colours will these fish see?

g Use your understanding of combinations to work out how many colours (both primary and secondary) the fish will see.

Questions

1. Bernie is putting up fairy lights to celebrate the New Year.
He has 5 different types of bulb that he can use:

- red flashing
- red
- green flashing
- green
- white.

What different combinations of bulbs could Bernie put in his string of fairy lights? List them all.

Answers to Lighting test

1. green and red   **2.** green and blue
3. red and blue   **4.** red, green and blue
5. red   **6.** red and green
7. blue and green   **8.** green
9. blue   **10.** red

Sound is like light

Sound and light carry energy

Sound and light both carry energy. Sound energy and light energy can both make things work. A microphone takes in sound energy and gives out electrical energy. In the same way, a **solar cell** takes in light energy and gives out electrical energy. Our eyes take in light energy and give out electrical energy that goes to the brain along nerves. Our ears take in sound energy and give out electrical energy, which also goes to the brain along nerves.

a Draw an energy transfer diagram for our eyes.

b Draw an energy transfer diagram for our ears.

Learn about

▶ Similar properties of sound and light

The solar cells take in light energy and give out electrical energy, which lights the bulb.

Sound is reflected or absorbed

Light is reflected from some surfaces and absorbed by others. Sound is also reflected from some surfaces. Reflected sound is called an **echo**. Some surfaces absorb sound. Snow absorbs sound. Sounds seem muffled when the ground is covered in snow. This is because there are very few echoes.

Some rooms are lined with materials that absorb sound. The recording studio in the photo is lined with sound-absorbing materials to prevent echoes, which might interfere with the recording. The ceilings of concert halls are also made of special materials to prevent echoes.

c Why do echoes need to be controlled in concert halls?

Different materials, different speeds

Sound travels at different speeds in different materials. It even travels at different speeds in air, depending on the conditions. Sound travels faster through warm air than through cold air, and faster in humid air than in dry air.

Material	Speed of sound in m/s
Air (at 0°C)	330
Water	1500
Wood (oak)	3850
Iron	5000

Light also travels at different speeds in different materials. Light travels at 300 million m/s in air, 92 million m/s in glass and 225 million m/s in water.

Look at the table showing the speed of sound in different materials.

d Maria looks at the table and decides that sound travels fastest in solids, slower in liquids and slowest in gases. What additional evidence should Maria collect to test her conclusion?

Refraction

Light refracts when it goes from air to glass, or water to air. This refraction happens because the light travels at different speeds in air, water and glass. Sound travels faster through warm air than cooler air. This means that sound will refract (bend) when it goes from warm air to cooler air, or cool air to warmer air.

On summer nights the air near the ground is cool and the air higher up is warmer. Some of the sound bends towards the ground, as shown in the top diagram. You get a similar pattern of refraction as light travels through different types of glass, as shown in the bottom diagram. Light that hits the boundaries at an angle refracts. Successive refractions bend the light into a curve.

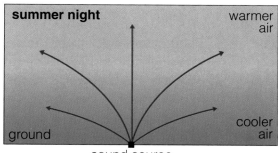

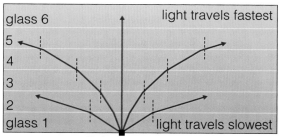

Pitch and colour

Objects that vibrate at different frequencies make sounds of different pitches, and we see light of different frequencies as different colours.

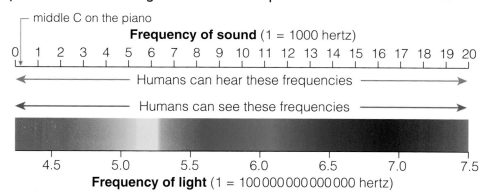

Loudness and brightness

Sounds can be loud or quiet. Large vibrations, with large amplitudes, make loud sounds. Small vibrations, with small amplitudes, make quiet sounds. Light can be brighter or dimmer. This is also related to amplitude. Very bright light has a larger amplitude than dim light.

e A note has a frequency of 1024 hertz. Is it above or below middle C?

f Is light with a frequency of 650 million million hertz orange or blue?

Questions

1. Copy and complete these sentences.
   a Reflected sound is called an ...
   b Pitch is like colour because ...
   c Brightness is like loudness because ...

2. **a** Sketch a diagram of what happens when light travels through six types of glass, slowing down more in each type of glass. Use the diagram above right as a guide.
   b Sketch a diagram of what would happen to the sound when there was warmer air close to the ground, with cooler air above it. This happens on a summer day.
   c When will sounds travel further close to the ground, during a summer night or a summer day?

For your notes

Sound and light carry energy.

Sound and light can be absorbed or reflected.

Sound and light travel at different speeds in different materials, so they can be refracted.

Sound and light can vary in frequency.

Sound and light can vary in amplitude.

Sound is different from light

Speed

Light travels very, very fast. Light travels through air at 300 million m/s. Sound travels much slower. The speed of sound in air varies, but it is about 330 m/s. In the time it takes for light to travel the length of a football pitch, sound would travel 0.1 mm.

Storms make both light, as lightning, and sound, as thunder. If a storm is 10 km away, the light from the lightning would reach you in 0.00003 s, while the sound from the thunderclap would take 30 s to reach you. The longer the gap between the lightning and the thunder, the further away the storm.

(a) Kyle is watching a storm. He sees lightning. After 3 s he hears thunder. How far away is the storm?

Measuring the speed of sound

Janet and Luisa are measuring the speed of sound. Janet goes to the other end of the playing field, measuring the distance with a measuring wheel. She ends up 300 m away from Luisa. Luisa has a large wooden clapper. Janet starts her stopwatch when she sees Luisa close the clapper, and stops her stopwatch when the sound reaches her. Janet measured 0.95 s.

Speed

To calculate speed you use this equation:

$$\text{speed} = \frac{\text{distance}}{\text{time}}$$

(b) Calculate the speed of sound according to Janet and Luisa's first experiment.

Janet and Luisa then do five other experiments. Their measurements are shown in the table.

Experiment	1	2	3	4	5	6
Time in s	0.95	0.98	1.04	0.92	0.98	0.96

(c) Why are the measurements different?

(d) Work out an average time for the sound to travel 300 m.

(e) Work out an average speed for sound from Janet and Luisa's experiment.

Measuring the speed of light

Measuring the speed of light is a lot harder than measuring the speed of sound. Light travels far too fast to use a stopwatch!

Albert Michelson was a famous scientist who measured the speed of light. He put a light source and a detector on the top of a mountain and a mirror on a second mountain. He measured the time it took for light to travel from the top of the first mountain, to the top of the second mountain and back again.

The mountains were 36 km apart and the light took less than 0.000 24 s to make the journey there and back! Obviously, Michelson could not use a stopwatch to measure 0.000 24 s – human reaction times are far too slow. Nowadays, he would probably use an electronic stopwatch controlled by a computer, but these instruments were not available in 1882 when Michelson was doing the experiments. Instead, Michelson made an ingenious timing device out of a spinning mirror with eight sides.

f The two mountains were 34 km apart. Why did the mountains have to be so far apart for the experiment to work?

Passing through

Light travels through any transparent material, or through empty space. Sound travels through solids, liquids and gases, but it cannot travel through empty space. Sound needs a material to travel through, but light does not.

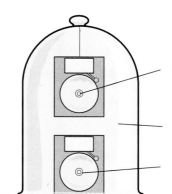

Bell **A** is hung from the top of the jar by a rubber band.

There is no air in the jar. All the air was pumped out.

Bell **B** is on the table.

g Think of three materials that sound can travel through but light cannot travel through.

h Look at the diagram of the two bells in a jar. Which bell would you hear? Why would you hear this bell, but not the other?

Frequency

Young people can hear sounds with frequencies between 20 hertz and 20 000 hertz. We see light with much higher frequencies. Red light has a frequency of 430 million million hertz and violet light has a frequency of 750 million million hertz.

Questions

1. Why do you see lightning before you hear thunder when a storm is far away?

2. Why does light travel through outer space but sound does not?

3. Sound is used to measure the depth of the sea. The boat sends out a sound, then measures the time before the echo comes back. Sound travels at 1500 m/s in water, so the distance the sound travelled can be measured.
   a The sound came back in 1 s. How far did the sound travel?
   b How deep was the sea?

For your notes

Light travels much faster than sound.

Sound needs a material to travel through. Light does not.

absorption   The process by which digested food passes through the lining of the small intestine into the blood.
When light or sound is soaked up by a surface, it is absorbed.

acid   A solution that has a pH lower than 7.

acid rain   Rain polluted by acidic gases such as sulfur dioxide dissolved in it. Acid rain is more acidic than rainwater that is not polluted.

aerobic respiration   The process by which plants and animals use oxygen from the air to break down their food to release the chemical energy from it.

air pressure   The gas pressure caused when air particles all around us hit us and other surfaces.

algae   Organisms that make their food using sunlight. Some algae are unicellular.

alkali   A base that dissolves in water, forming a solution with a pH greater than 7.

alternative   Alternative energy resources are energy resources that are not fossil fuels.

amino acids   Small molecules formed by breaking down proteins.

amoeba   A unicellular organism that feeds on other organisms.

anaemia   A disease caused by not eating enough iron or vitamin B12 in the diet, in which the person is pale and feels very tired.

anaerobic respiration   The process by which plants and animals break down their food to release the chemical energy from it, without using oxygen from the air.

angle of incidence   The angle between the incoming ray and the normal.

angle of reflection   The angle between the reflected ray and the normal.

annular eclipse   A solar eclipse in which a ring of light is seen around the shadow of the Moon on the Sun. The Moon is at its greatest distance from the Earth so its shadow is not large enough to cover the Sun completely.

anorexia nervosa   An eating disorder which causes a person to eat too little.

antagonistic pair   Two muscles that work against each other to move a bone at a joint. The muscles pull the bone in opposite directions.

anus   The opening through which undigested food passes out of the body.

aperture   A small opening.

artery   A blood vessel in which blood flows away from the heart.

arthritis   A disease of the joints, in which the joints become very swollen and painful.

artificial satellites   Satellites that are made by people.

asteroid belt   A zone between Mars and Jupiter where most of the asteroids in our Solar System are.

asteroids   Rocky objects in space. In our Solar System most of the asteroids are found in the asteroid belt.

astronomy   The study of planets, stars and other objects in space.

axis   An imaginary line through the Earth that runs from the North Pole to the South Pole.

balanced diet   A diet that has the right amounts of all the nutrients.

ball and socket joint   A type of joint that allows a bone to move around in all directions, as in the shoulder or hip.

basalt   An igneous rock with small crystals.

base   A substance that reacts with an acid and neutralises it.

battery   An object that changes chemical energy into electrical energy.

bimetallic strip   Two pieces of different metals joined together. One metal expands more than the other when it is heated, so the bimetallic strip bends.

biological washing powder Washing powder that contains enzymes to break down stains.

biological weathering Breaking down rock by the action of plants or animals.

biomass The total mass of a living thing, not including the water. Biomass can be used as an energy resource.

blood vessels Tubes in which blood flows all around the body.

calcium A metallic element. The mineral calcium is found in milk and cheese, and it keeps your teeth and bones healthy. The mineral calcium is actually calcium compounds.

calcium carbonate A basic compound present in some rocks such as limestone, chalk and marble.

canines Teeth for piercing and tearing meat.

capillary A very small blood vessel.

carbohydrates Nutrients found in foods such as bread, which give you energy.

carbon A non-metallic element present in fuels and in living things.

carnivore An animal that feeds on other animals.

cartilage A very smooth substance found on the ends of bones, which allows them to move over each other easily.

catalytic converter A device fitted to a car's exhaust that removes some polluting gases, such as carbon monoxide and nitrogen oxides, by chemical reactions.

cement A substance formed by chemical changes in the formation of sedimentary rocks, which joins the grains together.

chalk A type of sedimentary rock that contains calcium carbonate.

change of physical state Changing from a solid to a liquid or a liquid to a gas and back again.

chemical weathering The breaking up of rocks by chemicals in the environment. The substances in the rocks are changed into new substances.

chemicals Everything is made from different chemicals or substances. Chemicals can be elements or compounds.

chloride A salt that is made by neutralisation of hydrochloric acid.

cilia Tiny hairs on the outside of some types of cell.

circulatory system An organ system that transports substances around the body.

closed question A question that has only two possible answers, often 'yes' or 'no'.

coal Material from plants that lived many millions of years ago, used as a fuel.

cocoon A covering that a caterpillar spins around itself.

combination One way in which objects are put together.

comet A small object in the Solar System made of ice, dust and gas, that travels around the Sun.

compensation Making up for a change by balancing things out.

concentrated A solution that contains a lot of dissolved solute is concentrated.

concentration The amount of solute dissolved in a particular volume of a solution.

cones In animals – light detectors at the back of the eye which detect coloured light. In plants – structures that contain the seeds in conifers.

conifers Plants that reproduce from seeds in cones and have thin, needle-like leaves.

conserved When the same amount is there at the end as there was at the beginning. For example, when a solid is dissolved in a liquid, the mass of solution equals the mass of solid plus the mass of liquid. The mass is conserved.

constellation   A group of stars that form a recognisable pattern when viewed from a particular place on Earth.

consumer   An animal, that eats (consumes) plants or other animals.

contraction   A material getting smaller as it cools down.
When a muscle gets shorter, we say it is contracting.

corrosion   Eating away of the surface of a solid by a chemical reaction.

corrosive   Substances that may destroy living tissues on contact are corrosive.

crust   The outer layer of the Earth.

crystalline   A substance that contains crystals is crystalline.

cuticle   A waterproof layer on the surface of some leaves.

cyan   A colour of light produced by mixing blue and green light.

day   The time taken for the Earth to spin once on its axis.

decomposer   An organism that feeds on the dead bodies of plants and animals.

deficient   When something is lacking, for example, someone who does not eat enough of a particular vitamin is deficient in that vitamin.

delta   New land formed by deposition at the mouth of a river.

deposition   Small pieces of rock settling at the bottom of a river or the sea.

diffusion   Gas or liquid particles spreading out as their particles move and mix.

digestion   Process by which food is broken down into smaller molecules.

digestive system   The organ system that breaks down your food into smaller molecules and absorbs them.

dilute   A solution that does not contain much dissolved solute is dilute.

dioxins   Waste products of industrial processes, that are toxic.

disperse   Spread. Pollen is dispersed when it is spread to another flower, and seeds are dispersed to a new place to grow.

dispersion   The splitting of white light into colours.

donate   To give something, such as a healthy organ for transplant.

echo   A reflected sound.

ecosystem   An area such as a forest or a pond, including all the living things in it and also its soil, air and climate.

egestion   Passing undigested food out of the body.

electrons   Tiny particles that are found in an atom, outside the nucleus.

environment   The surroundings in a habitat.

enzymes   Proteins that speed up the breakdown of food in digestion.

epithelial cells   Special cells that make up the linings of your nose and throat. They make mucus to trap dust and germs.

equator   An imaginary line that goes around the middle of the Earth, midway been the North Pole and the South Pole.

equilibrium   A state of balance.

equinox   A day of the year when day and night are the same length. There is one equinox in the spring and another in the autumn.

erosion   Loose pieces of rock are broken down while being transported.

eruption   A volcano erupts when magma is forced out of it.

estimate   An informed guess, usually applied to numbers.

estuary   Where a river meets the sea.

ethanol   A substance produced by yeast as a product of fermentation. Ethanol is alcohol.

evaluate   To judge how good a model or experiment is, finding its good points and bad points.

expansion   A material getting bigger as it heats up.

extrusive igneous rock   Rock with small crystals, formed when lava cools quickly on the surface of the Earth, such as basalt.

faeces   The undigested food that is egested from the body.

fats   Nutrients found in foods such as butter, that give you energy and insulate your body.

fatty acids   Small molecules formed along with glycerol by breaking down fats.

fermentation   Anaerobic respiration carried out by yeast, which produces ethanol.

ferns   Plants that reproduce from spores and have leaves called fronds.

fertiliser   A substance used to keep soil fertile, so that plants have all the mineral salts they need to grow.

fibre   Bulky material found in cereals, fruits and vegetables which helps to keep food moving through your gut.

flower   An organ system in flowering plants that produces seeds.

flowering plants   Plants that reproduce from seeds made in flowers and have various shapes of leaf.

focused (in focus)   When an image is sharp rather than fuzzy, it is focused or in focus.

food chain   A diagram that shows how the organisms in an ecosystem feed on each other.

food web   Lots of food chains link together to form a food web, that shows the feeding relationships in an ecosystem.

forces of attraction   Pulling forces between particles, that hold them together.

formula   The ratio of different types of atoms in a compound.

fossil   The remains of an animal or plant that have been buried deep underground for millions of years and preserved.

fossil fuels   Materials from animals and plants that lived many millions of years ago, used as a fuel.

freeze-thaw   Water inside a crack freezes and expands, exerting a force on the rock. The ice then thaws. This process is repeated many times until the rock eventually breaks apart.

fronds   The large tough leaves of ferns.

fuel cell   A device that takes the energy released in a chemical reaction and turns it into electrical energy.

function   The job that something does.

galaxy   A collection of millions of stars held together by gravitational pull.

gas pressure   A pressure caused by gas particles hitting the sides of their container.

generator   A device that takes in kinetic (moving) energy and gives out electrical energy.

geocentric model   A model of the universe with Earth at the centre of the universe, and everything including the Sun moving around it.

geological time   Long periods of time, during which processes happen over millions of years.

geologist   A scientist who studies the Earth and rocks.

geostationary satellite   A satellite that orbits the Earth at the same speed as the Earth is spinning on its axis, so it stays above the same part of the Earth's surface.

geothermal   Heating by hot rocks under the ground.

glacier   A slow-moving river of ice which can erode rocks by scraping across the top of them.

global warming   An increase in the average temperature of the Earth.

glucose   A small molecule formed by breaking down carbohydrates, or made by plants in photosynthesis.

glycerol   A small molecule formed along with fatty acids by breaking down fats.

goitre   A disease caused by not eating enough iodine in the diet, in which the thyroid gland in the neck becomes very large.

grain   A tiny piece of material, such as sand.

granite   A type of igneous rock with big crystals.

gravitational force   The pulling force between one object and another. Gravitational force keeps objects in orbit around other objects.

guard cells   Special cells that are found either side of a stoma and can open and close it.

gullet   The part of the gut that links the mouth and stomach, also called the oesophagus.

gut   The long tube in your body down which food passes between the mouth and the anus, and where digestion and absorption take place.

habitat   A place where an organism lives, that provides all the things the organism needs to carry out the life processes.

haemoglobin   A chemical in red blood cells that carries oxygen around the body.

harmful   Harmful substances may have a health risk similar to but less serious than toxic substances.

heliocentric model   A model of the Solar System with the Sun at the centre of the Solar System and the planets moving around the Sun in circular orbits.

herbivore   An animal that feeds on plants.

hinge joint   A type of joint that allows a bone to move backwards and forwards.

hormone   A substance in the body that makes changes happen. Hormones may be given to farm animals, for example to make them grow.

humus   Dead animal and plant material found in soil. It provides plants with nutrients.

hydroelectric   Using the kinetic (movement) energy of falling water by changing it into electrical energy.

hydrogen   A non-metallic element that is an explosive gas.

igneous rock   Rock that is formed from molten lava or magma which has cooled and solidified.

image   An object seen indirectly on a screen or using a mirror or lens.

incisors   Teeth at the front of the mouth for tearing food.

indicator   A coloured substance that shows whether the solution being tested is acidic, alkaline or neutral.

intrusive igneous rock   Rock with large crystals, formed when magma cools slowly deep in the Earth, such as granite.

inverted   Upside down.

involuntary muscle   A kind of muscle that you do not consciously control.

iodine   A non-metallic element.
   The mineral iodine is found in fish, used by the thyroid gland to make a hormone that helps you grow.

iron   A metallic element.
   The mineral iron is found in liver and eggs, and it is used in your body to make blood.

irritant   Substances that can cause reddening or blistering in contact with the skin are irritant.

joint   A place in the skeleton where bones can move.

lactic acid   A substance produced by anaerobic respiration in animals.

large intestine   The part of the gut where waste food is stored and water is absorbed.

lattice arrangement   A regular pattern of particles found in a solid.

lava   Molten rock from deep below the surface of the Earth which reaches the surface through cracks or volcanoes.

leaf   A plant organ that is important for photosynthesis.

leap year   A year that has 366 days, that occurs every four years.

lens   A piece of curved, transparent material used to bend light.

ligament   Strong tissue that holds bones together at a joint.

lime   A basic substance containing calcium oxide, or other calcium compounds.

limestone   A type of sedimentary rock formed from the shells of sea creatures, which contains calcium carbonate.

line of best fit   A line drawn on a graph that shows the overall trend or pattern.

litmus   An indicator made from lichens.

luminosity   A measure of the light energy given out by bodies such as stars.

luminous   Objects that give out light are luminous.

lunar eclipse   An eclipse that occurs when the shadow of the Earth moves across the Moon.

magenta   A colour of light produced by mixing red and blue light.

magma   Molten rock found deep below the surface of the Earth.

magnesium   A metallic element.
   Magnesium compounds are needed by plants to make chlorophyll. These compounds are sometimes called mineral salts or nutrients.

marble   A type of metamorphic rock that is produced when limestone is heated under high pressure.

metamorphic rock   Rock formed when sedimentary or igneous rocks are changed by intense heat and/or pressure.

meteor   A very small piece of debris from a comet.

meteorite   A solid mass of rock or metal from space that lands on Earth.

methane   A hydrocarbon with the formula CH_4.

mineral salts   Salts dissolved in water in the soil that provide the elements plants need for growth.

minerals   All rocks are made up of substances called minerals. Different rocks are made up of different minerals or different mixtures of minerals.
   Compounds of calcium, iron, iodine and other elements that are needed in the diet in small amounts to keep your body healthy are also called minerals.

mitochondria   Small structures inside cells where respiration takes place.

Mohs scale   A scale used for measuring the hardness of a mineral.

molars   Teeth at the back of the mouth for grinding.

mosses   Small plants that look like a springy cushion. They reproduce from spores and have very small leaves.

mudstone   A dark grey sedimentary rock.

multicellular   A living thing that is made up of more than one cell is multicellular.

muscle   Tissue made up of muscle fibres that can contract.
   A muscle is an organ made up of muscle tissue along with other tissues such as capillaries.

muscle fibres   Bundles of long thin muscle cells, that make up muscle tissue.

natural gas   A gas formed from animals and plants that lived many millions of years ago, used as a fuel. It is mostly methane.

nervous system   An organ system that sends messages around the body.

neutral A substance that is neither acidic nor alkaline, with a pH of 7, is neutral.

neutralisation The chemical reaction that takes place when an acid reacts with a base.

neutrons Tiny particles that are found in an atom, inside the nucleus.

nitrogen A non-metallic element that is a gas present in the air.

non-luminous An object that does not give out light is non-luminous.

non-renewable A fuel (or other energy resource) that is not replaced as we use it is non-renewable.

normal An imaginary line at 90° to a surface.

northern hemisphere The top half of the Earth, above the equator.

nuclear A process or device that involves radioactive materials is described as nuclear.

nucleus The central part of an atom, made up of neutrons and protons.

nutrients Useful substances present in foods.

obese People who are very overweight for their height are obese.

object Something you look at using a mirror or lens to form an image.

oesophagus The part of the gut that links the mouth and stomach, also called the gullet.

oil A liquid formed from animals and plants that lived many millions of years ago, used as a fuel.

opaque A material that does not allow light to pass through is opaque.

open question A question that can have several possible answers.

orbit The path a satellite takes around the object it is travelling round.

organ A group of different tissues that work together.

organ system A group of organs that work together.

organ transplant A damaged or diseased organ is removed and replaced with a healthy one from an organ donor.

organic food Food that has been produced without using manufactured chemicals.

oxidation A type of chemical reaction. Adding oxygen is one type of oxidation reaction.

oxidised In an oxidation reaction, the reactant is oxidised.

oxygen A non-metallic element that is a gas. Oxygen is used in burning and in respiration.

partial eclipse An eclipse viewed from a place where the shadow is not complete.

particle theory A model that uses particles to explain why solids, liquids and gases behave the way they do.

penumbra An area of partial shadow where a partial eclipse is seen.

peristalsis Movements of the gut wall to push the food along.

pesticide A chemical used on crops to kill insects or other pests.

petal A plant organ that attracts insects to a flower.

pH scale A number scale used to measure the strength of acidity and alkalinity.

phases of the Moon The different shapes of the Moon seen as the Moon orbits the Earth.

phosphorus A non-metallic element. Phosphorus compounds (mineral salts) are needed by plants for growth.

physical weathering Breaking down rocks into smaller pieces, without changing them into new substances. Physical weathering can be caused by water, wind and changes in temperature.

pivot joint A type of joint that allows bones to move in a circular motion.

polar orbit An orbit that takes satellites over the poles of the Earth.

porous A substance such as a rock with lots of tiny holes in it is porous.

predator An animal that hunts other animals.

prey Animals that are hunted and eaten by predators.

primary colour One of the three colours of light that humans can see – green, red or blue.

producer A plant, that produces its own food by photosynthesis.

proteins Nutrients found in foods such as fish, used in your body for growth and repair.

protons Tiny particles that are found in an atom, inside the nucleus.

pupil The gap in the iris of the eye that lets light in.

quadrat A wooden frame measuring one metre on all four sides.

radioactive Radioactive atoms are unstable and break down, producing large amounts of energy.

random samples Taking samples from different places without choosing the places deliberately.

ratio A way of showing a scale factor. For example, a scale of 1:10 means you have to multiply your number or measurement by 10 to get the real measurement.

ray A thin beam of light.

recommended daily intakes (RDI) and recommended daily allowances (RDA) Levels set by the Government that advise about the amounts of different nutrients eaten each day.

red blood cells Special cells that carry oxygen around in your blood.

reflected When light or sound bounces off a surface, it is reflected.

refraction Bending of light when it travels from one material to another.

rejection This happens when a patient's body does not accept a transplanted organ and treats it as if it is something harmful.

relaxing When a muscle stops contracting and can be pulled back to its normal length, we say it is relaxing.

renewable An energy resource that is replaced as we use it is renewable.

reproduce To make more organisms of the same species.

reproductive system An organ system that is involved in reproduction.

respiration The process by which plants and animals break down their food to release the chemical energy from it.

respiratory system An organ system that takes oxygen into the blood and gets rid of carbon dioxide.

rickets A disease caused by not eating enough vitamin D in the diet, in which the bones are soft.

rock cycle A cycle that describes how the three rock types change from one to another over millions of years.

root A plant organ that takes in water and minerals, and anchors the plant in the soil.

root hair cells Special cells found in roots that are adapted to absorb water.

roughage Another name for fibre in the diet.

salt A substance formed in a neutralisation reaction.

sample A small part of something, used to represent the whole.

sandstone A type of sedimentary rock made up of grains of sand.

satellite An object that orbits a larger object.

scattered When light is reflected in many directions by a rough surface, it is scattered.

scrubbers   Devices that remove polluting gases such as sulfur dioxide from the fumes given out by power stations.

scurvy   A disease caused by not eating enough vitamin C in the diet, in which the gums bleed and the skin does not heal.

seasons   Times of different climate during the year. In the UK we have four seasons – spring, summer, autumn and winter.

secondary colour   One of the three colours of light produced by mixing two primary colours.

sediment   Small pieces of rock and dead living things which build up in layers at the bottoms of lakes or seas over millions of years.

sedimentary rock   A type of rock made up from layers of sediment that have built up over millions of years and become cemented together.

seeds   Structures used for reproduction in flowering plants and conifers.

shadow   Darkness due to an object blocking the light.

shale   A type of sedimentary rock formed from clay.

shutter   Something used to close an opening to stop the light coming through.

skeletal system   An organ system made up of bones. It protects and supports your body and allows you to move.

skeleton   Another word for the skeletal system.

slate   A type of metamorphic rock that has a layered structure.

small intestine   The part of the gut where enzymes and bile are added in alkaline conditions to digest the different substances in food. Absorption also happens here.

smog   A mixture of fog and smoke, or fog and other polluting gases.

sodium   A metallic element. A sodium salt is formed when sodium hydroxide neutralises an acid.

soil   A mixture of mineral grains made when rocks are broken up on the Earth's surface.

solar cell   A device that takes in light energy and gives out electrical energy.

solar eclipse   An eclipse that occurs when the Moon blocks the Sun's light from reaching the Earth. A shadow passes across the Earth.

solar energy   Energy given out by the Sun.

solar furnace   A device that concentrates thermal energy from the Sun and uses the thermal energy to heat a material.

Solar System   The Sun and the objects orbiting it, including Earth and the other planets.

solubility   A measure of how much of a solute will dissolve at a particular temperature.

source   Where something starts or is produced.

specialised   A cell that is adapted to carry out a particular function is specialised.

spectrum   The colours in white light – red, orange, yellow, green, blue, indigo, violet.

spores   Structures used for reproduction in mosses and ferns.

stem   A plant organ that holds the plant up and transports water and sugars.

stoma   A hole in the underside of a leaf that allows gases to move in and out.

stomach   The part of the gut where the food is churned up and mixed with enzymes in acidic conditions.

sublimation   Changing straight from a solid to a gas without becoming a liquid.

sulfate   A salt that is made by neutralisation of sulfuric acid.

summer solstice   The longest day, on 21 June in the UK.

synovial fluid   A liquid found inside joints that allows the bones to move easily.

synthetic materials Materials that have been made by people and which do not occur naturally.

tendon A tissue that joins muscles to bones.

tides The movement of water produced by the gravitational pull of the Moon. Tides can be used as an energy resource.

tissue A group of similar cells that carry out the same job.

topsoil The top layer of soil, made of tiny grains of rock and humus.

total eclipse An eclipse viewed from a place where the shadow is complete.

toxic Toxic means poisonous. Substances that may cause serious health risks and even death if inhaled, taken internally or absorbed through the skin are toxic.

toxic waste Waste that contains poisonous substances.

translucent A material that allows some light to pass through is translucent.

transmitted When light or sound passes through a material, it is transmitted.

transparent A material that allows light to pass through is transparent.

transported Moved to another place. Pieces of weathered rock may be transported by wind, glaciers or water.

turbine A device for changing movement in one direction into a spinning movement.

umbra An area of complete shadow where a total eclipse is seen.

unicellular A living thing that is made up of only one cell is unicellular.

universal indicator An indicator that has a range of colours showing the strength of acidity or alkalinity on the pH scale.

vegan A person who does not eat any animal products at all.

vegetarian A person who does not eat any meat.

vein In animals – a blood vessel in which blood flows back to the heart.
   In plants – a tube-like structure that carries water, mineral salts and food around the plant.

vertebrae Lots of small bones that make up your backbone.

villi (singular villus) Finger-like structures in the small intestine which increase the area for the absorption of digested food.

vitamin A substance such as vitamin C that is needed in the diet in very small amounts to keep your body healthy.

vitamin A A vitamin found in carrots that keeps your skin and eyes healthy.

vitamin B12 A vitamin that prevents anaemia.

vitamin C A vitamin found in fresh fruit and vegetables.

vitamin D A vitamin found in milk and butter and made in your body in sunlight, which gives you strong bones and teeth.

water A compound of hydrogen and oxygen. Water is the solvent in which all the chemical reactions in your body take place.

wave energy The kinetic (movement) energy of waves.

weathering Breaking rock down by chemical or physical processes.

wind energy The kinetic (movement) energy of the wind.

wind farm A large collection of wind turbines.

wind turbine A device that takes in the kinetic (movement) energy of the wind and gives out electrical energy.

winter solstice The shortest day, on 21 December in the UK.

year The time taken for the Earth to orbit the Sun.

yellow A colour of light produced by mixing red and green light.

Note: page numbers in **bold** show where a word is **explained** in the text. There are also definitions in the Glossary on pages **136–45**.

A

absorption
  of food **69**, 71, 136
  of light or sound **124**, 132, 136
acid 1–4, **2**, 5–7, 136
  and base *see* neutralisation
  in food 3, 7
  indigestion 3, 8
  and metals 12–13
  soil 9, 16–17
  and weathering 96
  see also hydrochloric acid; sulfuric acid
acid rain 7, 14–15, **15**, 81, 96, 97, 136
aerobic respiration **73**, **110**, 136
air
  pressure **56**, 136
  refraction in 126–7
  see also gases; pollution
algae **20**, 136
alkali and base 4–7, **4**, 9, 136
  and acid *see* neutralisation
  salt from 10–11
alternative energy **83**, 84–7, 136, 145
aluminium 12, 77
amino acids **70**, 136
ammonia 6, 7, 11
amoeba **20**, 136
anaemia **65**, 136
anaerobic respiration **73**, 136
angles of incidence and reflection **125**, 136
animals 63, 90, 106, 112–15, 140
  cells 20–1, 141
  fossil 92, 93, 139
  organs 19, 22–3
annular eclipse **39**, 136
anorexia nervosa **67**, 136
antagonistic pair **26**, 136
anus **69**, 136
aperture **123**, 136
artery **23**, 136
arthritis **25**, 136
artificial satellites 42–3, **42**, 136, 139
asteroid belt **32**, 136

asteroids **32**, 136
astronomy **36**, 136
atoms 46–7
attraction, forces of **50**, 58, 139
axis of Earth **38**, 136

B

balanced diet 66–7, **66**, 136
ball and socket joint **24**, 25, 136
balloons 56, 57
basalt **100**, 102, 136
base *see* alkali and base
battery **88**, 136
bimetallic strip **55**, 136
biological washing powder **71**, 137
biological weathering **95**, 137
biomass **84**, **113**, 137
blood
  cells **21**, 29, 73, 143
  vessels **22**, 23, 73, 137, 145
body 18–29
  map 28–9
  waste 69, 73, 113, 138
  see also blood; cells;
    muscles; organs; skeleton
boiling point **51**
bones *see* joints; skeleton
breaking point 61
burning 76–7, 80–1
butane 80

C

calcium **65**, 137
calcium carbonate **11**, 102, 137
  see also chalk; limestone
calcium chloride 11, 96, 137
calcium sulfate 11
cameras 122–3, 138
  parts of **123**, 136, 141, 144
canines **68**, 137
capillary **23**, 137
carbohydrates **64**, 66, 137
carbon 49, 80, **112**, 137

carbon dioxide 49
  and burning 81
  from chalk 11
  and neutralisation 9
  and plants 110, 111
  and respiration 22, 72, 73
carbon monoxide 47, 81
carnivores 114–15, **114**, 137
cars *see* vehicles
cartilage **25**, 137
catalytic converter **81**, 137
caterpillar 112–13, 115
cells 20–1
  animal 20–1, 23, 138, 143
  blood **21**, 29, 73, 143
  plant 20, 21, 138, 141
  and respiration 72–3
  specialised **20**, 144
cement **101**, 137
chalk 11, **103**, 137
change of physical state 50–1, **50**, 137
chemical energy 80, 82–3, 88
chemical weathering **14**, 15, 96–7, **96**, 137
chemicals **48**, 137
chlorides 10–11, **11**, 96, 137
chromatography 59
cilia **20**, 137
circulatory system 22–3, **22**
closed question **105**, 137
coal 76, 77, **78**, 80, 137
  electricity from 78, 83, 90–1
cocoon **112**, 137
cold *see* temperature
colours 5, 35, 128–31, 133, 138,
    (141–144), 145
  and frequencies 129
  and pitch 133
  see also primary; secondary
combination 130–1, **130**, 137
comet **32**, 137
communication satellite 43
compensation 16–17, **17**, 137
compounds 46, 48–9
concentrated **2**, **6**, 137
concentration **116**, 137
condensing 51

cones **109**, **131**, 137
conifers **109**, 137
conserved mass **58**, 137
constellation **36**, 138
consumer **114**, 138
contraction **26**, 54–5, **54**, 95, 138
copper sulfate 13, 58, 59
corrosion **12**, 138
corrosive **2**, **4**, 138
crust of Earth **100**, 138
crystalline **102**, 138
cuticle **108**, 138
cyan 130–1, **130**, 138

D

dams 86
datalogging 10
day **33**, 38, 41, 138
daylight hours 40–1
decomposer **115**, 138
deficient **64**, 138
delta **99**, 138
deposition **99**, 138
diesel 77, 80
diet *see* food
diffusion 52–3, **52**, 138
digestive system **23**, 68–71, **68**, 138
  digestion **68**, **70**, 74–5, 138
  enzymes **68**, **70**, 71, 138
  parts of **68–9**, 71, 139, 140, 142, 144
  peristalsis **68**, 142
dilute **2**, **6**, 138
dinosaurs 92, 93
dioxins **116**, 138
diseases 64–5, 67, 115
disperse **108**, 138
dispersion **128**, 138
donate **18**, 138

E

Earth 30, 32, 33, 44
  axis **38**, 136
  crust **100**, 138
  day **33**, 38, 41, 138
  orbit 42
  position 36–7
  size 33

Earth (continued)
see also year
echo **138**
eclipses **39**, 140, 142, 144
ecosystem **107**, 115–16, 138
egestion **69**, 138
electricity/electrical energy 88–9, 132
   and alternative fuels 83, 84–7
   and fossil fuels 78, 82–3, 90–1
electrons **47**, 138
elements 46, 48
energy 76–91
   alternative **83**, 84–7, 138, 145
   burning 76–7, 80–1
   food 66, **69**, 70–1, 72–3, 139
   geothermal **87**, 139
   kinetic 82, 85, 88
   nuclear **87**, 142
   renewable 84–6, **84**, 143
   solar **84**, 142
   thermal 80, 82, 83, 84, 85
   tidal **86**, 145
   for transport *see* vehicles
   see also electricity; fossil
      fuels; light; non-renewable
environment 106–19, **106**, 138
   see also animals; plants
enzymes **68**, **70**, 71, 74–5, 138
epithelial cells **20**, 138
equator **41**, 138
equilibrium **26**, 138
equinox **41**, 138
erosion **98**, 138
eruption **100**, 138
estimate **90**, 138
estuary **99**, 138
ethanol **73**, 77, 138
evaluate **44**, 139
evaporation 51
expansion 54–6, **54**, 95, 139
exploration satellite 43
extrusive *see under* igneous rocks
eyes 123, 129, 143

F

faeces **69**, 139
fats **64**, 66, 70, 72, 139

fatty acids **70**, 139
fermentation **73**, 139
ferns **109**, 139
fertiliser 11, **62**, 139
fibre (muscle) **26**, 141
fibre (roughage) **65**, 66, 139, 143
flower **23**, 108, 139
flowering plants **108**, 118–19, 139
focused (in focus) **123**, 139
food and nutrition
   absorption **69**, 71, 136
   acids in 3, 7
   balanced diet 66–7, **66**, 136
   chain **114**, 139
   for energy 66, 69, 70–1, 72–3, 137
   and environment 112–13, 114, 115
   organic 62–3, **62**, 142
   web **115**, 139
   see also digestive system; nutrients
forces of attraction **50**, 58, 139
forest *see* woodland
formula **49**, **79**, 139
fossil fuels 78–9, **78**, 139, 141
   and acid rain 14–15
   burning 80–1
   electricity from 78, 82–3, 90–1
   see also coal; natural gas; oil
fossils 78, **92**, 93, 109, 139
freeze-thaw **94**, 139
frequency 129, 133, 135
fronds, fern **109**, 139
fuel *see* energy
fuel cell **89**, 139
function **20**, 139

G

galaxy **35**, 139
gases 47, 80, 81, 110
   changes of state 50–1
   diffusion 52–3, **52**, 138
   molecules 48–9
   pressure 56–7, **56**, 139
   see also carbon dioxide; hydrogen;
      methane; natural gas; nitrogen;
      oxygen
generator **82**, 84, 85, 139
geocentric model **36**, 139

geological time **93**, 139

geologist **93**, 139

geology *see* rock

geostationary satellite **43**, 139

geothermal energy **87**, 139

glacier **98**, 139

glass 61, 125, 126, 133

global warming **80**, 140

glucose **70**, 140
    digestion of 67, 70, 71
    molecule 49, 70
    from photosynthesis **110**, 112, 113
    and respiration 72, 73

glycerol **70**, 140

goitre **65**, 140

grains **100**, 140

granite **100**, 102, 140

graphs 10, 58, 74–5

gravitational force 37, **42**, 86, 140

greenhouse effect 80, 140

guard cells **21**, 140

gullet (oesophagus) **68**, 140, 142

gut **68**, 140

H

habitat **106**, 108–9, 140

haemoglobin **73**, 140

hair relaxers 4

harmful **4**, 140

hearing *see* sound

heart 22, 23, 27

heat energy *see* thermal energy

heliocentric model **36**, 37, 140

herbivores 112–13, **112**, **114**, 115, 140

hexane 79

hinge joint **24**, 25, 140

hormones **62**, 140

humus **97**, 140

hydrocarbons 79
    see also fossil fuels

hydrochloric acid 6, 7, 10, 13, 102

hydroelectric power **86**, 140

hydrogen **12**, 13, **112**, 140
    as fuel 77, 88
    molecules 48–9

hydroponics **112**

I

ice 50, 94, 98

igneous rocks **100**, **102**, 140
    extrusive (and basalt) **100**, 102, 136, 140
    intrusive (and granite) **100**, 102, 140

image **122**, 123, 140

incidence, angle of **125**, 136

incisors **68**, 140

indicator **5**, 140
    universal **6**, 14, 145

indigestion, acid 3, 8

industrial effluent 9

insoluble 59

intestines 68, **69**, 71, 138, 141

intrusive *see under* igneous rocks

inverted image **122**, 123, 140

involuntary muscle 27, **68**, 140

iodine 61, **65**, 140

iron 12, **65**, 66, 140

irritant **4**, 140

J

joints **24**, 25, 136, 140, 142
    synovial fluid **25**, 144

Jupiter 32, 37, 44

K

kinetic energy 82, 85, 88

L

lactic acid **73**, 138

large intestine 68, **69**, 141

lattice arrangement **50**, 141

lava **100**, 140

leaf **23**, 140

leap year **40**, 140

lens **123**, 141

ligament **25**, 141

light and light energy 34–5, 80, 115,
    122–35, 138, 144, 145

lime 9, 15, 141

limestone 9, **96**, **101**, 103, 141
    weathering 14, 15, 96

line of best fit **74**, 75, 141

liquid 47, 50–1, 53, 138
    see also water

litmus **5**, 139
luminosity and luminous **35**, 141
lunar *see* Moon

M

magenta 130–1, **130**, 141
magma **100**, 141
magnesium 12, **112**, 141
marble 15, **103**, 141
Mars 31, 32, 33, 37, 44
mass, conservation of **58**, 138
matter 46–61
melting point 50, 51
mercury (metal) 54, 117
Mercury (planet) 32, 33, 42, 44
metals 12–13, 54, 112, 117, 140, 141
    bimetallic strip **55**, 136
    breaking point 61
metamorphic rocks 15, 100, **101**,
        102, 103, 141, 144
meteor **32**, 141
meteorite **32**, 141
methane 49, 61, 77, **79**, 84, 141
    see also natural gas
military satellites 43
minerals
    in food **65**, 141
    mineral salts **112**, 141
    in rocks **14**, **94**, 102, 141
mitochondria **72**, 141
models 44–5, 60–1
Mohs scale **102**, 141
molars **68**, 141
molecules 48–51, 70, 141
Moon 31
    lunar eclipse **39**, 141
    missions to 30, 42, 89
    phases of **38**, 142
    and tides 86
mosses **109**, 141
movement *see* kinetic energy
mudstone **101**, 141
multicellular **20**, 141
muscles and muscular system 21, 26–7, **26**,
        136, 140, 141, 143, 145
    fibres 26, 139
    heart 22, 23, 27

involuntary 27, **68**, 140
voluntary 27
music 120–1, 133

N

natural gas **78**, 79, 80, 81, 141
natural satellites 42
    see also Moon
navigation satellite 43
nervous system **23**, 141
neutral **5**, 7, 14, 142
neutralisation **8**, 9, 10, 15, 81, 142
neutrons **47**, 142
nitrogen 48, 49, 72, 81, **112**, 142
non-luminous **35**, 142
non-renewable energy **83**, 87, 142
    see also fossil fuels
normal 124–5, **124**, 142
northern hemisphere **40**, 142
nuclear energy **87**, 142
nucleus **47**, 142
nutrients 64–6, **64**, 142
    minerals **65**, 141
    plant **112**
    see also carbohydrates; fats; food; protein
nutrition *see* food

O

obese **66**, 142
object **122**, 142
observation satellites 42
octane 79
oesophagus (gullet) **68**, 138, 142
oil 77, **78**, 79, 80, 83, 142
opaque **126**, 142
open question **105**, 142
orbit **32**, 37, 42, 142
    polar **43**, 142
    of satellites 42–3
organic food 62–3, **62**, 143
organs and organ systems 19, 22–3, **22**, 142
    see also transplant
oxidation and oxidised **77**, 142
oxygen 48–9, **112**, 142
    and burning 77
    liquid (as fuel) 89
    and plants 110

oxygen (continued)
  and respiration 22, 72, 73

P

palaeontologists 92
partial eclipse **39**, 142
particles theory **46**, 142
  see also matter
peat 9, 109
penumbra **39**, 142
periscope 125
peristalsis **68**, 142
pesticide **62**, 142
petal **23**, 142
petrol 77, 80
pH scale **6**, 10, 15, 96, 142
phases of Moon **38**, 142
phosphorus **112**, 140
photosynthesis 110, 112, 113
physical weathering 94–5, **94**, 142
pitch and colour 133
pivot joint **24**, 142
planets 31–3, 35, 37, 42, 44–5, 61
plants 107, 112
  cells 20, 21, 141
  flowering **108**, 118–19, 139
  as food 112–13, 114
  fossil 109
  and green light 129
  habitat 106, 108–9, 140
  organs 23
  respiration 73, 110–11, 113
  vein **109**, 145
  see also soil
poisonous *see* toxic
polar orbit **43**, 143
pollution 9, 15, 81, 90–1, 117
  see also acid rain
porous **79**, **94**, 143
power stations *see* electricity
predator **115**, 148
pregnancy 67
pressure, gas 56–7, **56**, 136, 139
prey **115**, 143
primary colour **130**, 131, 143
prisms 128
producer **114**, 143
products 10–12

proteins **64**, 66, 70, 72, 143
protons **47**, 143
pulling forces 51, 61
pupil **123**, 143
pyramids of numbers 114

Q

quadrat **118**, 119, 143
questions 137, 142

R

radioactive **87**, 143
rain 94
  see also acid rain
random samples **118**, 119, 143
ratio 28–9, **28**, **118**, **119**, 143
ray **124**, 143
reactants 10–12
recommended daily allowances and
    intakes (RDA/RDI) **66**, 143
reflection/reflected 124–5, **124**, 129,
    132, 143
  angle of **125**, 136
refraction 126–7, **126**, 128, 133, 143
rejection **19**, 143
relaxing **26**, 143
renewable energy 84–6, **84**, 143
reproduce **108**, 143
reproductive systems 20–1, **23**, 108–9, 143
respiration **22**, 72–3, **72**, **110**, 143
  aerobic **73**, **110**, 136
  anaerobic **73**, 136
  plants 110–11, 113
respiratory system **23**, 143
rickets **65**, 143
rock 92–105
  cycle 100–1, **100**, 143
  erosion and deposition **98**, **99**, 138
  history 93
  minerals **94**, 102, 141
  properties 103, 104–5
  types *see* igneous; metamorphic;
    sedimentary
  see also weathering
root **23**
  hair cells **21**, 143
roughage (fibre) **65**, 66, 143

S

salt 10–12, **10**, 143
    mineral **112**, 141
    in solution 58, 59
sample/sampling **29**, 90–1, **90**, 143
    random **118**, 119, 143
sandblasting 95
sandstone **101**, 103, 143
satellites **42**, 143
    artificial 42–43, **42**, 136, 139
    see also Moon
saturated 58, 59
Saturn 32, 37, 44
scattered light **125**, 143
scrubbers **81**, 143
scurvy **64**, 143
seasons **40**, 41, 143
secondary colours 130–1, 130, 136, 139,
    141, 143, 144
sediment **99**, 144
sedimentary rocks **100–1**, **102**, 103, 137,
    141, 143
    see also limestone
seeds **108**, 109, 144
seeing *see* eyes; light
shadow **122**, 144
shale **103**, 144
shutter **123**, 144
skeleton and skeletal system **24**, 144, 145
    see also joints
slate **101**, 103, 144
small intestine 68, **69**, 71, 144
smell 52
smog **81**, 144
sodium 11, 144
sodium chloride 10, 11, 81
sodium hydroxide 4, 6, 7, 10, 11, 81
soil **14**, **97**, 144
    acidic 5, 9, 16–17
    alkaline 5
    humus in **97**, 140
    mineral salts **112**, 141
    topsoil **97**, 145
    see also plants
solar cell **89**, **132**, 144

solar eclipse **39**, 144
    annular **39**, 136
solar energy **84**, 144
solar furnace **84**, 144
Solar System 30–7, **32**, 144
    see also Earth; Moon; planets
solids 46, 50–1
solstices **40**, 41, 144, 145
solubility 58–9, **58**, 144
    solution *see* acid
solvents 58, 59
sound 120–1, 132–4
source **122**, 144
space 30–1, 42, 44–5, 89
    see also Solar System; stars
specialised cell **20**, 145
species 108–9
spectrum **128**, 144
speed of light/sound 132
spores **109**, 144
starch 70, 71, 74–5
stars 34–5, 41
    constellation **36**, 138
steam 51, 82
stem **23**, 142
stings 9
stoma **21**, 144
stomach **68**, 69, 144
sublimation **61**, 144
sulfate **11**, 144
sulfur dioxide 14, 15, 81
sulfuric acid 2–3, 11, 12, 13
summer solstice **40**, 41, 144
Sun 34, 36–7
    energy from *see* fossil fuels; solar
    heliocentric model **36**, 37, 140
synovial fluid **25**, 144
synthetic materials **78**, 145

T

teeth 68, 137, 140
telescope 35, 37
temperature (heat and cold)
    and changes of state 50–1
    and diffusion 53
    and pressure 56–7, 60
    and refraction 133

temperature (continued)
  and solubility 58–9
  of stars 35
  and weathering 95
  see also contraction;
  expansion; thermal energy
tendons **26**, 145
thermal energy 80, 82, 83, 84, 85
thermometer 54
tides **86**, 145
tissue 21–2, **21**, 145
  see also muscles; organs
toothpaste 8
topsoil **97**, 145
total eclipse **39**, 145
toxic **2**, **4**, 116–17, 138, 145
  waste **116**, 145
translucent **126**, 145
transmitted light or sound **128**, 145
transparent **126**, 145
transplant, organ 18–19, **18**, 142
  rejection **19**, 143
transported **98**, 145
turbines **82**, 84, 85, 145

U

umbra **39**, 145
unicellular **20**, 145
universal indicator **6**, 14, 145

V

vegetarian and vegan **67**, 145
vehicles 15, 77, 81, 88–9, 117
veins **23**, **109**, 145
Venus 32, 33, 35, 42, 44
vertebrae **25**, 145
villi (*singular* villus) **69**, 145
vitamins A, C, D and B12 **64–5**, 66, 145
voluntary muscles 27

W

washing powder **71**, 137
waste
  from body 69, 73, 113, 138
  energy 83
  gases 80, 81, 110
  toxic **116**, 145

water treatment 9
water 143
  from burning 80
  changes of state 50–1, 137
  and deposition 99
  electricity from 86, 140
  and erosion 99
  in food **65**, 66
  molecules 48–9
  neutral 7, 14
  and plants 110
  and refraction 127, 128
  and respiration 72, 73
  solubility 58–9
  waste 9
  and weathering 94
wave energy **85**, 145
weather 43, 80
weathering 94–7, **94**, 145
  biological **95**, 137
  chemical **14**, 15, 96–7, **96**, 137
  physical 94–5, **94**, 142
wind
  energy **85**, 145
  farm **85**, 145
  turbine **85**, 145
  and weathering/erosion 95, 98
winter solstice **40**, 41, 145
woodland and forest 15, 107, 108, 109–11, 114

Y

year **33**, **40**, 145
  leap **40**, 141
yeast 73
yellow 130–1, **130**, 145

Z

zinc and acid 12–13

The authors and publishers would like to thank the following for permission to use photographs:

Cover photos: Ostriches, Tony Stone Images. **Colourful Windmill**, Science Photo Library/Martin Bond. **Volcanic Eruption**, Oxford Scientific Film/Hjalmar R. Bardarson.

1.1d, **1.2b**, **1.2c**, Andrew Lambert. **1.2f**, Collections/Sophia Skyers. **1.2g**, Wildlife Matters. **1.3a 1–7**, **1.4a**, **1.4b**, Andrew Lambert. **1.4d**, Garden & Wildlife Matters. **1.5a**, Peter Gould. **1.5c**, **1.5e**, **1.6a**, **1.6b**, **1.7b**, Andrew Lambert. **1.7c**, Environmental Images/John Morrison. **1.7e**, Andrew Lambert. **1.7g**, SPL/Simon Fraser. **1.7i**, Environmental Images/Ron Barnes. **2.1b**, Popperfoto. **2.1c**, Tony Stone/Manoj Shah (Pigs) Robert Harding. **2.2d**, **2.2e**, Corbis. **2.3a**, SPL. **2.4a**, SPL/John Daugherty. **2.4b**, SPL (knuckle – D. Roberts) **2.4e**, SPL/Clinical Radiology Dept. Salisbury District Hospital. **2.5a**, SPL/Quest. **2.5e**, Action Plus (Glyn Kirk, Neil Tingle). **3.1b**, SPL/PLI. **3.1c**, SPL/Novosti. **3.1e**, SPL/NASA. **3.2b** SPL/Space Telescope Institute, NASA, NASA coloured by Mehau Kuluk, US Geological Survey, NASA, Space Telescope Science, Institute/NASA, NASA, NASA, NASA, NASA. **3.3a**, SPL/Jerry Mason, Andrew McClenaghan, Amy Trustram Eve. **3.3b**, SPL/Pekka Parviainen. **3.3c**, SPL/Space Telescope Institute/NASA. **3.4b**, **3.4c**, SPL. **3.4d**, SPL/Dr Jeremy Burgess. **3.4e**, Mary Evans Picture Library. **3.5b**, SPL/Dr Fred Espenak. **3.7c**, **3.7e**, SPL/European Space Agency. **4.1b**, SPL/Sheila Terry. **4.1g**, IBM Corporation, Research Division, Almaden Research Centre. **4.2a**, Andrew Lambert. **4.4a**, **4.4b**, **4.4c**, **4.4g**, **4.4h**, Andrew Lambert. **4.4i**, Robert Harding. **4.5a**, Andrew Lambert. **4.5d**, SPL/David Nunuk. **4.6a** Tony Stone Images/Randy Wells. **4.6d**, **4.7a**, **4.7c**, Andrew Lambert. **4.8c**, Peter Gould. **4.8d**, Barnaby's Picture Library. **4.8e**, **4.8f**, Andrew Lambert. **4.8g**, Peter Gould. **5.1a**, Tony Stone/Mark Segal. **5.1b**, Holt Studios/Phillip Mitchell, **5.1c**, **5.1d**, Holt Studios/Nigel Cattlin. **5.2a**, **5.2b**, **5.2c**, **5.2d**, Andrew Lambert. **5.2g**, SPL/John Paul Kay, Peter Arnold. **5.3c**, The Stock Market, Robert Harding. **5.3e**, SPL/Oscar Burriel, **5.3f**. Action-Plus/Glyn Kirk. **5.4d**, SPL/Eye of Science, Juergen Berger, Max-Planck Institute. **5.6g**, SPL/Andrew Syred. **6.1d**, Andrew Lambert. **6.1f**, Tony Stone/Yvette Cardozo. **6.1g**, Tony Stone/Lorne Resnick. **6.1l**, Action-plus/Andy Willsheer. **6.1m**, Popperfoto. **6.1n**, **6.1o**, SPL/NASA. **6.2a**, Andrew Lambert. **6.3d**, Environmental Images/Matt Sampson. **6.4a**, Environmental Images. **6.5a**, Holt Studios/Nigel Cattlin. **6.5b**, Environmental Images/David Hoffman. **6.6b**, Tony Stone/Robert Cameron. **6.6d**, Environmental Images/John Novis. **6.6f**, Environmental Picture Library/Clive Shirley. **6.7a**, Fiat. **6.7d**, Associated Press/Steve Holland. **6.7g**, SPL/Martin Bond. **7.1a**, **7.1b**, Natural History Museum, London. **7.1c**, **7.2a**, **7.2c**, GSF Picture Gallery. **7.2e**, S Nicholson. **7.2f**, Environmental Images/Trevor Perry. **7.3a**, GSF Picture Library/Robert Harding/Roy Rainford. **7.3b**, Andrew Lambert. **7.3c**, **7.4a**, GSF Picture Library. **7.4b**, Environmental Images/Clive Jones. **7.4c**, **7.4d**, **7.5b**, **7.5c**, **7.5d**, GSF Picture Library. **7.6b**, **7.6c**, **7.6d**, **7.6e**, **7.7c**, **7.7d**, **7.7e**, GSF Picture Library. **8.1a**, News Team International/Mike Sharp. **8.1c**, Garden & Wildlife Matters. **8.1d**, Robert Harding/Adam Woolfitt. **8.2a**, SPL/Simon Fraser. **8.2b**, Wildlife Matters. **8.2c**, Garden Matters/Steffie Shields. **8.2d**, SPL/Simon Fraser/Eye of Science. **8.2e**, SPL/ Simon Fraser/Claude Nuridsany & Marie Perennou. **8.2e**, Garden Matters. **8.2f**, SPL/Alex Bartel/John Howard. **8.3a**, Garden & Wildlife Matters. **8.5a**, Oxford Scientific Films/David & Sue Cayless. **8.7c**, Andrew Lambert. **9.1c**, SPL/Martin Dohrn. **9.2b**, Andrew Lambert. **9.3f**, SPL/David Scharf. **9.3g**, Trevor Hill. **9.4a**, **9.4b**, **9.4f**, Andrew Lambert. **9.4j**, Bruce Coleman Collection/Kim Taylor. **9.5a**, SPL/David Parker. **9.5b**, SPL/ Pekka Parviainen. **9.5d**, Robert Harding/Tim Hall. **9.5e**, SPL/Adrienne Hart-Davis. **9.6a**, SPL/Vaughn Fleming. **9.7a**, Andrew Lambert. **9.7e**, Redferns/David Redfern. **9.8a**, SPL/Kent Wood.

The publishers have made every effort to trace copyright holders, but if they have inadvertently overlooked any, they will be pleased to make the necessary arrangements at the first opportunity.